This is a great tool for leadership programs and home bible studies. Mike has extraordinary revelation about building both the new and mature Christian into the Great Commission. The book shows a unique process that mirrors how Jesus matured his disciples—students growing into servants, and the diagrams provide a great breakdown of the steps to be taken for this excellent growth.

—Patricia Medina, Bible Teacher

Impressive and from the heart. I love the concepts. I pray that the book affects many people & churches!

—Michael Hodge, Lakewood Church

This book sets the standard; the small group aid you've been looking for. More than a book, this gift of love provides the "must-have" techniques for spiritual growth.

—AJ Baltes, PhD Communication Studies

This book gives practical insight into God's work in lives and can help refocus wandering Christians. It clearly explains how the Lord makes disciples, and helps us better understand our role in his plan.

—Kirby Wiseman, Bible teacher

A well done, living, functional roadmap of the process of spiritual growth, maturity and service.

—Mike Bianchi, CEO, Win Association
Founder, Legacy Coach International

This book is the map to follow. It should never be on a shelf! It belongs in full view to serve as a reminder of what a Christian walk with God is all about.

—Katherine Koch, Sun Corp.

This book brought revelations about my spiritual growth and my relationship with the Father.

—Doug Truong, Consultant

This well written book will bless, feed, and teach you.

—Maurice Harrell, Minister

From Speak to Share

To MONICA Lowe,
May you be blessed
beyond your imagination,
filled beyond your dreams,
and used beyond your
abilities. May God grant you
favor on the internet!
Mike Marburger
FAVOR BEYOND
MEASURE!

Michael Marburger

From Speak to Share

How God Builds a Christian

TATE PUBLISHING & *Enterprises*

Published by Tate Publishing & Enterprises, LLC
127 E. Trade Center Terrace | Mustang, Oklahoma 73064 USA
1.888.361.9473 | www.tatepublishing.com

Tate Publishing is committed to excellence in the publishing industry. The company reflects the philosophy established by the founders, based on Psalm 68:11,
"The Lord gave the word and great was the company of those who published it."

Book design copyright © 2010 by Tate Publishing, LLC. All rights reserved.
Cover design by Kandi Evans
Interior design by Kellie Southerland

Published in the United States of America

ISBN: 978-1-61566-772-7
1. Religion, Christian Life, Spiritual Growth
2. Religion, Bibical Studies, General
10.02.22

Dedication

I dedicate this book to those desiring to understand the process that God uses to reach them, change them, grow them, and return them to fellowship with him through the blood sacrifice of Jesus Christ, which provides eternal life. This return is followed by his constant infusion of growth and wisdom, displaying to others that God is firmly Lord of their lives.

I dedicate this book to those servants desiring to reach others and be used by God to effect growth and to those who desire to know the framework that God uses to accomplish growth. This includes pastors, preachers, teachers, students, Bible-based counselors, mission leaders and participants, Bible study leaders, Sunday school teachers, evangelists, and those seeking to fulfill the Great Commission.

Acknowledgment

I want to first thank God, then those he used to bathe me in truth, and finally those he used to support me as I walked his path to author and polish the text in this book.

To our heavenly Father, I humbly and joyously stand in worship for all of the truth that he revealed to me for the book and for all of him that waits in the text, desiring to surround, touch, and change readers. He touched me with so much truth that I sometimes wonder if some of what he shared with me fell off of my plate, never getting to the keyboard. I trust, though, that he reminded me again—said it in a different way, and I remembered and included that wonderful morsel of truth.

I want to thank my brother in Christ and counselor friend Gary Lynn of Family Christian Counseling Center in Houston, Texas. Gary, you were used by the Lord so many times to frame my thought-life to line up with truth revealed in the scriptures. This book would not be what it is without your being a clean vessel of God which allowed him transform me by the renewing of my mind. Thank you my dear friend and brother in Christ.

I want to thank my pastors, Joel and Victoria Osteen, and the staff and teachers at Lakewood Church. Their teachings are a river of life flowing from the throne of God. Those teachings watered me, carried me, and planted me for service. Dr. Paul Osteen, thank you for your encouragement, as we discussed the sixteen points of this book in your office. You embraced those points so quickly and energetically that I was even more convinced that the message was powerful and needed to be published. Dodie Osteen, thank you for your positive encouragement and for reminding me that I have not, because I have not asked, and that when I ask God, he delights in answering. Pastor Todd, thank you for steering my life and steering my efforts towards Tate Publishing.

I want to thank the people in the Lakewood Church fellowship group who meet in my home. God used you to show me even more that his Word works and that people who desire to grow and who saturate themselves in the truth can release old wounds, embrace change, grow, and blossom into even more mature followers of Christ. I am so honored to know you and even more honored to be in fellowship with you. Thank you, fellowship group.

I want to thank those whom God sent to be proofreaders of this text: Violet, Terri Lois, Gary L., Gary G., Doug W., Doug T., Joanne, Delena, Love Lea, Donna, Maria, Eric, Patricia, Michael, AJ, Kirby, Michael B., Michael H., Katherine, Maurice, Linda, Dianna, Chantel, and Tracey. Each of you are aware of the clarifications that God used you to illuminate. I am so humbled by your service to God in the way your feedback improved the readability of the message in this text. Thank you Terri Lois, your suggestions changed the book the most, improving readability and impact. Thank you, Violet for letting God move you to quickly read the earliest proof copy. You shared that you had no time to read, yet you became my first responder. Your excitement blessed and inspired me when you emailed me at midnight, sharing that you could not put it down and had just six pages left to read. Jim, although you were not a reader, God used you to sharpen my focus on salvation.

I want to thank Tate Publishing, whose constant positive encouragement made it be a pure joy to work with them, as we both served God by getting this book to those desiring to hear the message God intended to be published.

Foreword

We read plainly in the Gospels that Jesus' words give us a mandate to go into all the world and make disciples of all people. It is no mystery that we are living in an age of biblical illiteracy, and our families, our cities, our nation, and our world all need Jesus today—now more than ever. The gospel of Jesus Christ is the only thing that can transform people from darkness into the light. As a pastor and missionary, I am faced with this transformation challenge every day. As I lead people to Christ, I realize the journey has only just begun. How does God build disciples? How does He use us to lead people into a devoted relationship with Christ, so they can walk in the true authority that Christ imparted to us when he sent our helper the Holy Spirit?

I believe this book reveals in such simple terms, sixteen steps to maturity as a Christian—from student to servant leader. Whether you're just starting your journey as a Christian, or you're looking for new ways to lead people through the discipleship process, Michael Marburger's, *From Speak to Share: How God Builds a Christian* takes you on a journey into a Holy Spirit-inspired tutorial of understanding that transformation challenge.

The author has a passion for teaching and a perspective that only comes from the very fabric of who God created him to be. Thank you, Michael, for being obedient, as the Lord led you to write this book, and thank you for reminding us that if God is going to use us to be disciple makers, we have to allow him to do the work through us. Thanks for being a disciple making follower of Christ!

—Todd B. Hull
Pastor of Koinonia and The Journey Ministries
Lakewood Church – Houston, Texas
Co-Founder: Tower of Hope Ministries

Table of Contents

Diagrams

Poems

Introduction

"God, how will you use me to reach the hurting and walking wounded?" I was quiet in spirit in the midst of that storm when he spoke, and I will never again see counseling situations the same. I was praying about issues that God had put before me. He was using me to offer faith-filled words to some hurting people. They wanted my help to work through some of their life problems.

Man may think, but wisdom and revelation come from God.[1] All good and perfect gifts come from God.[2] God speaking through us[3] is always a wonderful thing, whether it is a prophetic utterance, a profoundly good sermon, or just a single Word.

"Man plans his path but the Lord directs his steps."[4] My conclusion had always been that this scripture passage refers to life events expressed with words, such as vocations, vacations, churches, businesses, banks, homes, cars, finances, and even mates. God has shown me *steps* and *processes*, which steer man in his spiritual growth and measure the progress of that growth. Truth clearly beacons out that the growth of man is directed by the Lord,[5] when it tells us that Paul plants, Apollos waters, but growth comes from God.[6] Spiritual growth starts by hearing God. In quiet times, we hear the still small voice of wisdom—that is quietness of Spirit not the quietness of events. We can hear him in the storm, if our spirit is quiet and listening. The sower sows the seeds,[7] and we can only pray to be good soil, when the seed touches us and tries to take root, hoping it will produce good fruit.

I asked him, "*Father, what do I let you say or do through me to reach this hurting person?*" In his gentle voice, God began to share with me. I began to write, and when I finished writing, there before me were eight words—penned with an unusual indent—that excellently describe the "ordered *steps* of a man" progressing in stages from non-believer to maturing believer. Eight words! I marveled at their simplicity, smiled that they rhymed, worshiped that they were profound, and pursued them, because they fed my spirit. Like any Word from heaven, the longer I soaked in it, the more revelation poured through it.

I studied these eight words to let revelation soak into me. A few days later, he gave me a question to ask him. Only God—only God!—can so perfectly give us revelation, watch us grow in it, and then invite us to question him, so he can share more. The first eight words were still developing within me and I was not expecting anything new. I heard that still, small voice recognize that the eight words described man's walk, but they were all man responding to God. I heard that still, small voice blare out with the loudness of a trumpet and the softness of a feather. "*But what does God do for man to respond with these eight steps?*" Immediately, I picked up the question, as if I had thought of it myself. In total unprepared innocence, I offered the question to God: "*Father, what do you cause to happen such that man responds with these steps?*" I freely offer to all concerned that the answer I received was not within my mind to manufacture. I am convinced, though, that it was in the mind of God, and he shared it with me to help many.

Once again, in his quiet voice, God spoke eight more words, and in obedience I wrote them with the same unusual indent as the first. As I read this fresh, newly received second set of eight words, I giggled at their simplicity, laughed in joy at their beauty, and worshiped at their majesty. Wisdom and clarification came, as I prayed and studied the Word of God, reflecting on what he wanted me to see in them. They also rhymed and were quickly collected together with the first eight into two columns of eight words with that same unique indent. I began to see it as a method with two processes. I began to see the left column as a process of eight *steps*, which God initiates and the right column as our proper response. This has matured into an awareness of the right column being the *student process* to identify the activity of learning and growing toward God and the left column being a *servant process* to identify being an empowered vessel of God.

As opportunity presented itself, I shared this method with others, and they expressed amazement. I think that only God can be so simple yet so profound. As an example, consider creation and the hydrogen atom, which is simple yet profound, not fully comprehended, but trusted. The atom—with a proton and an electron—is a basic building block of all structures in our universe. Every galaxy is built from combining and extending the proton and electron-building blocks. Only God can set up something so finitely small that builds something so infinitely large, simple, and profound—simply profound. All truth from God offers the same banner, simple and profound, which is somewhat understood at the finitely small and barely comprehended at the infinite, let alone heavenly. In John 3:12, Jesus said, *"I have spoken to you of earthly things and you do not believe; how then will you believe if I speak of heavenly things?"*

Servant/student is a fair general description, yet a much richer understanding comes from soaking. The value of this book is enhanced by study and revelation. This book first shares the *student process* of eight *steps* that we grow through that takes us from nonbeliever to maturing believer. The *steps* for *student* are: *hear, believe, ask, receive, do, care, show,* and *share.* These *steps* take the *student* through the first commandment to love God.[8] Following the *student process* is the *servant role,* the second process of eight *steps.* God initiates these *servant steps* to allow us to grow through the *student process.* The *steps* for *servant* are: *speak, caress, offer, bless, teach, mend, empower,* and *send;* and they exemplify God fulfilling the second commandment through the *servant.*

We are challenged to consider where we are in either the *student process* or the *servant process* and how God desires to move us to the next *step.* There are many areas of life, so we may be in different *steps* in various areas of our lives. God has a purpose for your life—a calling for service to him. He desires to build you and prepare you so you can respond to that calling. With that calling in mind, see if you can identify your position or progress in either the *student process* or the *servant process*.

Notice that the *student process* and *servant process* can be seen as the same two that Jesus Christ shared. The purpose of life is to love God with all of our heart, mind, soul, and strength (go vertical) and then love your neighbor as yourself (go horizontal). The *student process* is vertical. It is about beginning and maturing our relationship with our heavenly Father. The *servant process* is horizontal. It is about reaching out to others but only after the relationship with your heavenly Father is matured by the *student process*. God will not call a person to minister, unless he has prepared them and empowered them to do so. Those unprepared cannot carry the Word of God; they cannot contain it and will tend to trample it under their feet.[9]

Revelation understanding of these processes must come from God. There may be more understanding to come, yet I believe that I am to share what he has given me. At first as I shared this dual process with others, I was unaware of the power of the truth buried in the method. As others affirmed the wisdom in it, I am convinced that what is shared here is truth from God. My desire is that wisdom overtakes you, as you invite understanding of these *steps*, their interrelationships, and how God will be drawing you to your next level of growth in his kingdom.

As truth in these chapters energizes the reader, the Holy Spirit may offer additional scripture passages to support or magnify a point stated or even illuminate new revelations about a position not presented here. You are invited to give glory to God, take notes, and to bask in his growth. You are encouraged to seek truth presented here, embrace it, grow at God's rate for you, and develop into a servant of the living God.

A note about italicized words in the text

The appendix notes a number of terms used in the text which are part of the processes documented in the book. A judgment was made concerning presentation of these terms in italics. Presenting them in italics causes reading of the text to become busy at times, but not presenting them in italics can allow the reader to miss the significance and depth of the processes in many parts of the text. The choice was made to go with italics for terms representing the processes.

A note about scripture passage references

Scriptural truth from the Word of God is used extensively throughout the text of this book. This truth is the basis of support for positions stated. Scripture passages referenced are placed as endnotes at the end of the book. The New International Version (NIV) of the Bible is used unless otherwise noted, such as the Message and Living Bible translations.

The purpose of each sentence in this book is to enhance understanding and build revelation. In each case of scripture reference, a judgment was made regarding readability and understandability. Clarification on those judgments is as follows:

1. Sometimes an entire scripture passage is quoted in the sentence to enhance understanding of the revelation of the position stated. In those cases, the scripture passage is quoted in the sentence and the source parenthetically referenced, such as *"Hear me that your soul may live"* (John 8:47). Passages quoted verbatim are not additionally included as endnotes.

2. Sometimes it would be distracting to combine a quote of a full scripture passage in the same sentence along with the position stated. That combination would cause the sentence to be so busy that the reader could miss the revelation that the sentence is meant to communicate. In these cases, the scripture passage is in the endnote, unless it falls into the category below.

3. In some sentences, the scripture reference is so extensive that the reader would need to access the New International Version (NIV) for themselves. An exam-

ple is the reference made to creation in Genesis. Reader revelation of that truth will be enhanced by reading that passage of scripture, but the extensive quotation is not presented in the book. In these cases, the suggested passage is referenced parenthetically, i.e., (Read Genesis 1).

In referencing some scripture passages in the endnotes, the author will draw attention to the truth that is being illuminated.

Joshua 1:7
Caretakers of the truth: Be strong and very courageous. Be careful to obey all the law my servant Moses gave you; do not turn from it to the right or to the left, that you may be successful wherever you go.

When multiple verses are referenced, such as Mark 4:13–20, the entire reference is presented in the endnote as one text to read.

To preserve integrity of Biblical text in the endnotes, scriptural passages are presented as printed in copyrighted Biblical text, without regard to punctuation. This method leaves some passages appearing unfinished and grammatically deficient, but honors the passage. Ellipses are used in the passage quotes to indicate the quote does not start at the beginning of the verse, end at end of the verse, or to indicate the break between non-contiguous verses quoted.

Audience

This book describes a method God uses to build Christians. A diploma proves education but not necessarily *wisdom*. God touches those he chooses to touch. Being aware of the method described here does not automatically empower one to use the information wisely. Wisdom must come from God because Paul plants, Apollos waters, but growth, wisdom, and empowerment come from God.[10] This book is for believers and non-believers. It is for students, counselors, ministers, prayer warriors, and teachers who desire to learn and understand this method of how God builds Christians. It is for pastors and other servants of God and for parents seeking to raise Godly children. It is for those who aspire to reach others with the truth of the gospel of Jesus Christ. It is for those seeking to understand methods supporting God fulfilling the Great Commission through us, and for those seeking to improve their effectiveness in reaching others with the gospel of Jesus Christ; the gospel of truth.

This book can help families grow into Godly places of safety. Jesus Christ clarified that the purpose of life is to love God with all we have and to love others as ourselves.[11] Genesis 2:24 clarifies that marriage is between man and woman when it says, *"For this reason a man will leave his father and mother and be united to his wife, and they will become one flesh."* Malachi 2:15 clarifies that the purpose of marriage is to produce godly offspring when it says, *"Has not the Lord made them one? In flesh and spirit they are his. And why one? Because he was seeking godly offspring. So guard yourself in your spirit, and do not break faith with the wife of your youth.*" This book describes a framework for reaching people, including spouses and children,[12] for the kingdom of God. This book outlines the method for building Christians, for building believers, and for building Godly offspring. You are invited to grow in knowledge, understanding, and wisdom as you read *From Speak to Share: How God Builds a Christian.*

Student Process:

Learning to Love God

In fulfillment of the first commandment,[13] the *student process* guides us through eight *steps* that address our love and honoring of God. It is here that we learn to love God and where *"Love the Lord your God with all your heart, mind, soul, and strength"*[14] is birthed and matured. During this time, the *student* goes from weak belief in God's truth to strong belief and is *transformed* by the actions of God. We are challenged to consider where we are in these *steps* in the various parts of our lives. God moves in the *student* to cause them to

Hear		God's truth in God's way;
	Believe	God's truth;
Ask		God for that truth to be personalized into their life;
	Receive	God's response;
Do		What God's truth requests;
	Care	For that truth intentionally until a *Transformation* takes place;
Show		The *Transformation* by a *changed* life and mindset; and then
	Share	The new truth openly with others.

Each *step* of the *student process* is cumulative and durative. When completed, each *step* is a foundation for the next *step*. If a foundational piece crumbles, the *student* is in danger of sliding backward in faith, faltering, or representing our Father in a less-than-excellent manner. Everyone grows at a different rate through the eight *steps* of the *student process*.

Diagram 1—The Student Process
God sends students through a progression of steps so they can learn his truth.
Copyright 2010 Michael Marburger

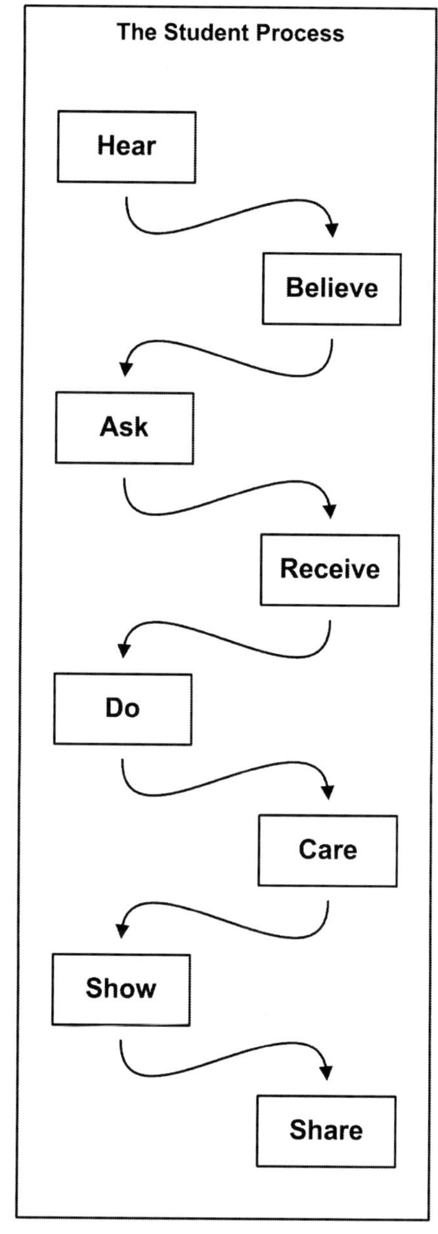
The Student Process
Hear
Believe
Ask
Receive
Do
Care
Show
Share

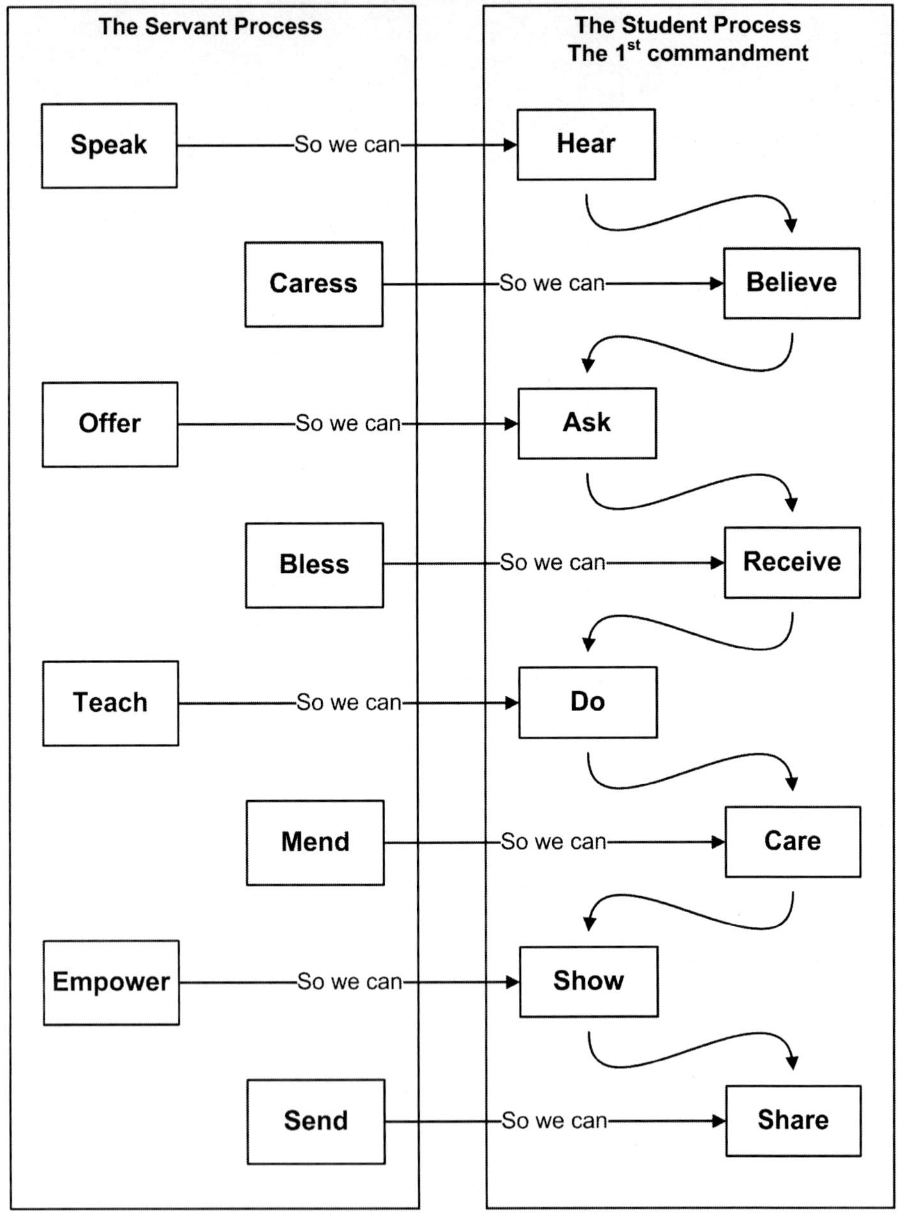

Diagram 2—God Serving the Student
Psalm 127:1 "Unless God builds a house, they that build labor in vain…"
God builds his children by serving and teaching them. He is the ever present help in time of need. We must mature to be what he wants us to be.
Copyright 2010 Michael Marburger
The Servant Process
The Student Process
The 1st commandment
Speak
So we can
Hear
Caress
So we can
Believe
Offer
So we can
Ask
Bless
So we can
Receive
Teach
So we can
Do
Mend
So we can
Care
Empower
So we can
Show
Send
So we can
Share

Hear

Assertion about Hear

We begin our lives in the flesh. The flesh does not *believe* the things of the Spirit, and the flesh cannot perceive the truth. Hearing is a spiritual perception of God's truth not related to eardrums. There is truth in heaven—truth and no deception. Deception was expelled from heaven. Jesus tells us he saw Satan, the deceiver, fall like lightning.[15] Since there is truth and only truth in heaven and deception is among us, we live amidst deception. When we overcome the world and *believe* the truth from heaven—even though we cannot see it—that is faith. Faith does not come by human intellectual understanding, because even children can have faith.[16] Faith is being absolutely convinced of the truth from heaven, even though we cannot see it.[17] "Saving Faith" is being convinced of the saving truth of the sacrifice of Jesus Christ, even though we cannot see it.

The Journey of Hear

Prayer helps prepare hearts to *hear*. In Isaiah 55:3, the Word says, *"Hear me that your soul may live."* The journey toward a life of serving God, our Maker, begins with *hearing*. Jesus said, *"Let him hear."*[18] We are not commanded to *hear*. We are given the opportunity to *hear*. We get to choose to *hear*. Romans 10:17 tells us that, *"Faith comes by hearing the message and the message is heard through the word of Christ.*" Restated using the description of faith above, Romans 10:17 expands to b*eing absolutely convinced of the truth in heaven, even though we cannot see it comes by hearing the truth of the message of Christ.* The message of Christ is that God loves us and wants us to understand that Jesus paid the price to restore us to fellowship, because our heavenly Father desires the relationship with us that we were originally created to have.[19]

Romans 10:17 presents that faith comes by *hearing* the truth from heaven; *hear* is the first *step*. The parable of the Sower[20] clarifies to us that the first response to a God-sent word is to *hear*. Our growth is determined by what we *believe* and what we *do* after we *hear*. We can *hear* the truth and then:

1. Have it stolen by the one who comes to steal, kill, and destroy.[21]

2. Avoid planting it deeply, thus lose it soon.

3. Avoid making it a priority in our lives and crowd it out.

4. Allow God to cause it to produce good fruit.

Miracles Associated with Hear

When we *hear*, the miracles of God are present to both convince and *celebrate* the *hearing*.[22] These are miracles of God where we have a need and God provides his remedy. God has left the ninety nine sheep,[23] so he could pursue us to get us to *hear* his truth and respond.

The Journey That is Distant from Hear

It is possible to hear the truth and have great fruit,[24] but what about those who do not *hear*?

1. It is possible to be unable to *hear*.[25]

2. It is possible to be in rebellion where the enemy can cause one to ignore the opportunity to *hear*.[26]

We must be open to *hear*. Since faith comes by *hearing*,[27] *hearing* must be first. The Parable of the Sower in Mark 4:13–20 clarifies to us that we can *hear*, and then by our actions and priorities, we let it become fruitful or fruitless.

Blockages to Hear

Hearts and attitudes hardened by the enemy and his agents can be filled with all manner of deception and confusion, making it difficult to *hear* truth. Calloused hearts can close ears. Closed eyes can prevent perception. The root of not *hearing* and of missing any of God's perfection, which is sin, is being deceived by untruth or affected by events that Satan has caused. Socialization by unbelieving families, peer groups, and societies tend to teach us to revel in the flesh and focus on only the flesh. This is exemplified in Mark 10:4–5 where Jesus revealed the origins of divorce, as it is written: "*They said, 'Moses permitted a man to write a certificate of divorce and send her away. It was because your hearts were hard that Moses wrote you this law,' Jesus replied.*" Soft hearts don't pursue divorce. Soft hearts yield to God's way. Soft hearts seek to *hear* God and his truth.

Pride is another sin that can block a person from *hearing* God. The stubborn and broken *student* figuratively plugs their ears to ensure that they do not have to *hear* what they have already chosen to ignore. This is indicative of the mindset of, "I cannot be wrong, I've already made a decision." As an example, perhaps you've seen children plug their ears because they do not wish to *hear* any additional information about a topic.

Not all sin closes the heart to *hearing*. In Genesis 4:9 after Cain killed Abel, he could still *hear* God *speak* to him. Cain was in denial about his sin when he responded to God's questioning with, "*I don't know, am I my brother's keeper?*" but it is clear that he could still *hear* God's confrontation.

The Journey toward Hear

God must cause this growth.[28] The *student* must get a *revelation* from God that they need to *hear* and then *desire* to *hear*. Prayer helps prepare hearts to *hear*. *Hearing* alone is not enough, but it is the beginning of the *student process* of growth. When we *hear* truth and obey it we are *blessed*.[29] There is more in the effort beyond *hearing*; we must go through *believe*, *ask*, and *receive* to get to the *step* of obedience, which is *doing*. When you *hear* God's voice, obey, even if it does not make sense,[30] but be cautious that you are *hearing* God *speak* and not the enemy.[31]

How Do We Start to Hear?

The *student* must *invite* this *step*. We must be open to *hear*. We *hear* in our spirit, and it opens our eyes and ears of faith. We must have a soft heart. When Jesus cured the wilted hand in Matthew 13:15, as he said, *"For this people's heart has become calloused; they hardly hear with their ears, and they have closed their eyes. Otherwise they might see with their eyes, hear with their ears, understand with their hearts and turn, and I would heal them."*

Changing the Heart to Hear

Set your heart towards listening to whatever God says through his scriptures. Verify your understanding through people you trust spiritually. Every church wants to proclaim that they are *speaking* truth; wars have been fought over the differences. The measuring stick used by Jesus Christ was that the blind see, the lame walk, the sick are healed, the deaf *hear*, the dead are raised, and the poor have good news preached to them.[32] Find and submit your heart to a church that is changing lives in these dramatic ways and you will be exposed to truth.

Trouble has a way of opening ears. This happens when a situation gets so rough that the conclusion is that only a higher power can address it, such as sickness, divorce, unemployment, persecution, or natural disaster. During trouble, some hearts are softened and run to God.[33]

Find a place where God is moving to see his real miracles. Miracles have a way of opening ears. Many bible-based, bible teaching churches are seeing *transformed* lives, and are good and trustworthy havens of growth. The need is to *hear*, and God has a provision that can be found at institutions.

The Challenge to Hear

The *student* must not only *permit* but also *embrace* and be *changed* by the *hearing step*. Are you open to *hearing* God's truth?[34] Are you good soil ready to produce good fruit one hundred fold? Are you so busy with things of the world that the truth is crowded out, or are you willing to *hear* truth?[35] Is someone trying to *speak* truth to you? Are you in *hear* mode? Ask God if there is an issue that he is trying to *speak* to you about, you are not *hearing*, or your *hearing* is not producing fruit one hundred fold. Is there something that comes to your mind right now? The solution is to pray that God causes you to become good soil for his truth.

If you have not yet *accepted* the sacrifice of Jesus Christ as Savior and Lord, giving you access to the Father and someone is talking with you about this truth, consider the need to *hear*. Let that truth settle into your spirit. Do not spend time looking for a higher power or authority; there is none.[36] There is no better deal. *Hear* what God is saying to you. Think about this life-saving truth being presented to you. There is nothing of value to lose and everything of value to gain. God tells us in Isaiah 55:3, "*Hear me, that your soul may live.*" *Hear* him, trust him, and let him prove to you that he is what he says he is and will do what he says he will do.

If you are a believer and God has someone talking with you about a truth that is difficult to *hear*, go to the Father and go to scripture to *seek* out wisdom and understanding. Spend time praying and fasting to *seek* out the truth. Trust God to show you the truth to *hear* and do not reject it. Truth is in his Word. Study that truth over and over and over, until *revelation* pours forth and your heart becomes soft towards it. Give that truth time in your life, until you *hear* its message.

Promotion beyond Hear

Promotion from God will not come until the *student celebrates* the growth and *worships* God as the changer. At this time of promotion, the *student* has been exposed to God's truth and—beyond the physical—has *heard* in their spirit. Because they have *heard*, they have succeeded in this opportunity to get closer to God and growing into his plan for their lives.

God desires that the *student seek* him for the next *step* of growth, which is to *believe*. The *student* has *celebrated hearing*, and now God wants them to get the *revelation* of the need to *believe*. He will take action to promote that *revelation* in the *student* and will wait.

Reflections and Discussion

Please reflect on the questions presented in the section titled "Main Discussion Guide for the Student Process," on page 194. Additionally, the following questions focus on *hear*:

1. What does Isaiah 55:3 mean where it says, *"Hear me that your soul may live."*?

2. What happens when one hears about salvation through Jesus Christ?

Believe

Assertion about Believe

We *believe* the truth,[37] as written and revealed[38] to us by God.[39] We *believe* in Jesus Christ as Savior.[40] We are not to *believe* every spirit but to test what is being said against the Word of God.[41] *Believing* was such a powerful life-*changing* event, that in Acts, the followers of Christ are referenced as *Believers*.[42] Even the demons believe.[43]

When we absolutely *believe* truth from heaven, even though we do not see it *yet*,[44] that is faith. With that definition, "*Pray in Faith*" expands to "*Pray absolutely believing the truth in heaven, even though we do not see it yet.*" Pray not just because it is written in the Bible; pray because it is written on your heart. Pray not just because it is written on your heart but because it is truth from God. Truth existed before creation. Truth frames creation and thus defines the universe. The universe was still rumbling from creation, when truth from God was already fixed as immutable, unchangeable, undeniable, and infallible. *Believe* it! *Speak* it!

You are God's ambassador as you walk through life situations. If you do not pray in *faith*, perhaps no one else will either. Command it in the name of Jesus. Command it, because you are a child of the most high God. Jesus gave us authority[45] over the enemy who is a liar and the father of lies.[46] Command it with the authority that you have been given, just like Jesus did as he spoke to the demons.[47] Use

Jesus as your example. Command it, because you are God's child. This is the power that the Father desires us to appropriate. It is not originating *within* us, it is appropriated *by* us. It belongs to the Father, and he delights in us using his truth to restore his creation. You are not manufacturing this truth; you are only agreeing with the Father *about* his truth. In Matthew 18:18–20, Jesus said,

> *I tell you the truth, whatever you bind on earth will be bound in heaven, and whatever you loose on earth will be loosed in heaven. Again, I tell you that if two of you on earth agree about anything you ask for, it will be done for you by my Father in heaven. For where two or three come together in my name, there am I with them.*

Truth encourages us to get with some other person to agree in prayer about an issue. We are to stand together *believing* and God will act.

The Journey of Believe

We cannot *believe* what we have not *heard.* We cannot *believe,* unless we are fertile soil. After we have *heard,* we have a choice to *believe* or not to *believe.* We have to be prepared by God to even *believe.*[48] God uses many vehicles to prepare a heart to *believe.* Some hearts are prepared sociologically by God through their families, friends, and acquaintances, telling them about Jesus and living out that faith. Some hearts are prepared by joy in the heart. Some hearts are prepared by a complete breaking down of life, until there is nothing left except to reach out to the Father in heaven, and from the perspective of that broken heart, it appears that there is nothing to lose by *believing.*

God is the preparer of hearts, but the *hearer* is the one who must decide to *believe.* The key is to not lean to your own understanding,[49] but to ask the Holy Spirit to help you consider the question, *"Should I believe this?"* God sometimes waits for the heart to be prepared prior to confronting us with a call to *believe.* In 2 Samuel 11–12[50] God did not use Nathan to confront David at the moment of sin, but waited at least 9 months until Bathsheba bore the child. 1 Corinthians 7 tells us that an unbeliever exposed to a believer who is living out the Lordship of Jesus Christ can prepare the heart to *believe*.[51] There is a time for everything under the sun,[52] and at any moment, either immediately upon *hearing* or any time later up until death, we can make the choice to *believe* the truth based upon what we have *heard*.

Miracles Associated with Believe

Believe in the Lord Jesus and you shall be saved, you and your household.[53] In Matthew 9:27–29,[54] Jesus healed the blind, after he confirmed that they *believed*. The Message interprets verse 29, as "*Become what you believe.*" The New International Version translates verse 29 as "*According to your faith will it be done to you.*" Faith begins in that *step* of *believing*, and both translations present that if you *believe* the truth from heaven, miracles can and do occur.

In Luke 8, the woman who had been bleeding for years *believed* that if she just touched the garment of Jesus Christ, she would be healed.[55] She touched the garment and was instantly healed. In Matthew 8:2, the man with leprosy *believed* when he came before Jesus and said, "Lord, if you are willing, you can make me clean." Jesus touched him and healed him.

The Journey That is Distant from Believe

A disobedient life style displays a life twisted by unbelief. Hebrews 3:15–19[56] indicate that some *hear* and rebel instead of *hearing* and *believing*. Verse 19 indicates that they could not enter God's rest because of their unbelief, and verse 18 calls that disobedience. When we disobey, we are not in *belief*. We must *believe* in order to get to the next *step*. Not *believing* leaves us stranded in a sea of disobedience-related actions, until the moment when we drop our pride and *believe* the truth that *transforms*.

Read Isaiah 30:1-9 for an example of the nation of Israel being distant from *believing*. God chastises them for going to Egypt for protection, instead of him, and concludes in verse 9 calling them, "children unwilling to listen," then in verse 12, indicates that they have "rejected this message."

Blockages to Believe

Deception is from the liar and father of lies.[57] Deception can occur before we *hear* truth or after we *hear* truth, and when it is either not deeply planted or if we are not good soil. Confusion comes from knowing the truth and being confronted with deception in such a way that we are pulled away from faithful steadfastness. Confusion can be defined as knowing the truth but *believing* something that is not truth.

Sociology teaches us that the family is the primary agent of socialization. If our family teaches us that green is red and someone approaches us with the corrective truth, the truth may be unrecognizable because of our current belief system. A life infected by enemy-influenced people may produce conclusions not authored by our heavenly Father, and when one *hears* the truth, the truth may be too foreign to *believe*.[58]

Confusion is a blockage to *believing* God's truth. *Believing* deception puts up a roadblock to *believing* God's truth, because deception and truth actively oppose each other. There is a resistance to *believing* the truth when we believe and really own the crippling lies of the enemy. Consider the child who hears all of his life that he is nothing and worthless or that God and the church are just frauds and this is reinforced by parents living out a corrupted lifestyle. When this message is combined with a culture of pursuing alternate happiness, the child can grow to resent God, who loves him, and become resistant to *believe,* because of a durative impactful deception. This is an example of deception before the person could even *hear* the truth.

The Journey toward Believe

God must cause this growth. The *student* must get a *revelation* from God that they need to *believe* and then *desire* to *believe*. Prayer helps prepare hearts to *believe*. God will do just about anything to get us to *believe* his truth, whether it is a sending a miracle, a life-storm, or his Son dying to get our attention. There are two realms of activity that affect the ability to *believe*: the physical realm, and the spiritual realm.

In the physical realm, I am convinced that two actions, and two actions only, will succeed. Those two must be initiated by someone anointed by God, and they are: *speak* and *caress*. *Speak* and *caress* (presented later in this book) are actions that share the truth in love and do it in the same way God *speaks* to us with that still, small voice, which is a voice of gentle, persuasive love. The same gentle persuasiveness must be used in counseling sessions by the gifted, anointed counselor. That method does not scare away but *offers* acceptance, safety, and nurturing.

In the spiritual realm, pray in faith. This is prayer that *believes* truth. It stands in the gap for the *student*. This prayer never lets go, never gives up; it hammers[59] heaven's door, agreeing with God and praying for the *student* to become fertile soil. The dedication to allow God to *change* the *student* causes the *servant* to fast for them and agree with two or more other solid *believers* about them. God desires the *student* to *believe* so much that they prepare room in their life for the results.

How Do We Start to Believe?

The *student* must *invite* this *step*. In Mark 9:23–24,[60] the man understood it correctly when he said, "I *believe*, help my unbelief!" God is our helper in faith. Ask God to help this lack of ability to *believe*. He delights in restoring faith. He delights in healing the wounded heart and soul. He delights in preparing hearts and watching them turn to him in realization that they have fallen short and that they are accepted with open arms.[61] God is the source of *believe*. He will make *belief* and praise spring up from all nations.[62]

Changing the Heart to Believe

Only God can *change* the heart to *believe* mode.[63] Every person has free will and gets to choose. Only God can supernaturally arrange situations in a person's life, so they can choose to *believe*. The heart cannot *believe* truth without the assistance of God. As an example, Paul did not *believe* the truth about Christ until he was touched by God on the road to Damascus.[64]

The Challenge to Believe

The *student* must not only *permit* but also *embrace* and be *changed* by the *believe step*. If you have not yet *accepted* the sacrifice of Jesus Christ as Savior and Lord, giving you access to the Father, know that God wants you to *believe* him. When the truth is *believed*, the spirit of deception is defeated. "*A man believes in his heart and confesses with his lips and thus is saved.*"[65] Jesus said to us, "*You shall know the truth and the truth shall set you free.*"[66] *Believing* the truth is a major turning point in salvation. *Believe* God!

If you are a *believer* and God has *sent* someone to open up a truth to you, God wants you to *believe* him[67] through them. Work on *accepting* by faith not works.[68] *Believe* the scriptures as written and revealed and Jesus Christ as Lord. You are to be his witness and *servant* whom he has chosen. Ask him if there some area of your life where you have *heard* but not fully *believed*. Are you willing to let God grow you through this to get to the next *step* of maturity in him? What fruit is there from *believe*? What fruit are you producing? Is your fruit from God?

Promotion beyond Believe

Promotion from God will not come until the *student celebrates* the growth and *worships* God as the changer. At this time of promotion, the *student* has *believed* God's truth. He is another *step* closer to being *transformed* by that truth. There has been no outward manifestation of that act of *believing*, but it is still a valid and true experience.

God desires that the *student seek* him for the next *step* of growth, which is *asking*. The *student* has *celebrated believe*, and now God wants them to get the *revelation* of the need to *ask*. He will take action to promote that *revelation* in the *student* and wait.

Reflections and Discussion

Please reflect on the questions presented in the section titled "Main Discussion Guide for the Student Process" on page 194. Additionally, the following questions focus on *believe*:

1. What happens when one believes that Jesus could be Savior and Lord?

2. Read Matthew 9:29 (Message). "*Become what you believe.*" What does this scripture passage mean to you? What happened when Adam believed the wrong thing in Genesis? Is there anything you have *believed* that is not from God and that he would like you to allow him to *change*?

3. What are blockages to *believing*, what might cause them, and what might minimize them? Are there any in your life?

4. What are some examples of hearing but not *believing*? Are those happening in your life?

5. What does it mean for you to *believe* God so much that you act on what you have *believed*?

Ask

Assertion about Ask

The next *step* of growth after *hear* and *believe* is to *ask* for what God has promised.[69] We *ask*[70] for what God desires to *bless* us with,[71] [72] as revealed in scripture and by the Holy Spirit.

God has given us the ability to choose freely. Our loving Father never forces anything upon us but works and woos us until we are fertile soil and until we are prepared to *ask*. The *step* of *ask* is precious and vital, because it evidences our *desire* for what the Father has prepared for us in his glory.[73] The phrase so many may remember is that we must *ask* Jesus Christ into our heart and lives, "Jesus, I *ask* you into my heart to be my Savior and Lord."

The Journey of Ask

The act of *asking* is indicative of *desire*. 1 Corinthians 1:18 says, "*The message of the cross is foolishness to those who are perishing, but to us who are being saved it is the power of God.*" Those *hearing* God's truth and considering it foolishness have no *desire* for it, but those who *hear* truth and *believe* it, follow-up with a request for what they *believe*. Certainly the most important follow-up is *asking* for eternal life through the sacrifice of Jesus Christ on the cross. Several versions of the Scriptures translate 1 Corinthians 1:18 as a future event in process: "being saved." This "being saved" in verse 18 is "in the process of being saved" or "on the way to being saved," as well as afterwards when we are sure of the truth. The *step* of *ask* is in the category of "on the way" to being saved. Using the *student process* of this book, salvation would not be firm until *receiving* occurs in the next chapter.

Miracles Associated with Ask

The miracle of *asking* is that God moves. God moves to answer his people whom he loves. Prayer moves the hands that rule the world.[74][75] God answering prayer always seems like a miracle, because we observe heavenly provision. When Jesus spoke to his disciples about *asking*, in Luke 11:9, he said, that God moves when we *ask*.

The Journey That is Distant from Ask

Jesus said that the message of the cross is foolishness to those who are perishing.[76] Those who are being deceived have wandered from the choice to *ask*. The opportunity is still there, they have just not seen the truth enough or enough of the truth to *seek* it and *desire* it. We will find him when we *seek* him with all our heart.[77]

Living a life calloused by hardness of heart prevents us from *asking* and *seeking*. Hardheartedness is a result of work by the enemy. All good and perfect gifts come from God;[78] hardheartedness does not. Pride puts blinders over our spiritual eyes which permits us to wander aimlessly down a path leading to destruction.[79]

Blockages to Ask

Consider the three statements below:

1. *"I am not worth it. I hear and believe, but just cannot ask for this gift. I am not worth it. I've tried in the past but failed so many times. I am not going to try again."*

2. *"I created this problem; I'll handle it myself."*

3. *"I believe in Jesus, but I don't need him to get involved in my business dealings or my personal life."*

Each of these statements reveals a heart that is hardened or deceived. Enduring a life of brutality or deception coming through another person establishes belief systems that do not promote *asking* for benefits freely *offered* by God. These broken hearts may have been infected by the enemy and are convinced that they must earn the right to *ask* for a free gift, that they must fix the problem themselves by excluding God, or that God is not interested in being Lord of every area of their lives. Actually, it is during these times that *asking* is most important, lest the life continue down the wrong path to destruction.

The enemy of our souls may convince some that the *asking* fell on deaf ears at the throne of life and their request was to no avail. The truth is that God cannot lie[80] and desires for all to *receive* what he *offers*. However, if we *ask* to spend it on our own passions, we *ask* outside the will and plan of God, and we will not *receive* what we *ask* for.[81] Be neither too bold nor too timid; limit your requests to the banquet provided by God:[82] *seek* no more or no less than what God desires for you. When you are sure of what God desires for you *ask* with confidence and enthusiasm.

The Journey toward Ask

God must cause this growth.[83] The *student* must get a *revelation* from God that they need to *ask* and then *desire* to *ask*. Prayer helps prepare hearts to *ask*. One cannot *ask*, unless one *believes* what they have *heard*. They must *ask* for growth.

How Do We Start to Ask?

The *student* must *invite* this *step*. We *ask* for God's promises with peace and assurance, because the truth has convinced us that he desires to give us what he promises. Boldness is not required;[84] neither is timidity. Thankfulness is always appropriate. Consider being attacked by sickness, and someone approaches you with a cup of liquid that would heal you instantly. The *offering* person is so excited to give you the cup that they can hardly stand still. They wiggle in joy at the opportunity to meet your need, and you can see their enthusiasm. The cup is *offered*, but you must reach for it, which in this example is to *ask*. Boldness and timidity are out of the picture. All that is required for *asking* is an understanding that the giver delights in your *acceptance* of the cup. We *ask* with thanksgiving in our heart.

Another example that might illustrate the mindset of *asking* is having someone you love being held hostage and being terribly mistreated. You encounter someone who can have them set free. He is dancing around in excitement, and you can tell that he is all but begging for your *permission* to set your loved one free; but he just needs your signature. To make it easier, all he needs for you to do is *ask* for the release of your loved one. Begging, boldness, and timidity are just not in the equation, only heartfelt thanksgiving from you. Just *ask*, "*Will you give me what you promise? Thank you!*"

Changing the Heart to Ask

God will use his *servant* in his way to touch his loved ones who are being held hostage and being terribly mistreated. The hurting heart has already *heard* and *believed*, and waits at the door of *ask*, holding onto the baggage of the past, which is corruption and deception from the enemy. A miracle that is needed now is one that causes us to feel worthy enough, entitled enough, and valuable enough to *ask* for his *blessing* and our entitlement. It is an entitlement, because it is his truth, his truth is his Word, and his Word is his promise.

The Challenge to Ask

The *student* must not only *permit* but also *embrace* and be *changed* by the *asking step*. Is there something that you *believe* God for that you do not have?[85] Do you have not, because you have *asked* not?[86] Are you *seeking* more from your heavenly Father? Visualize the truth that he is dancing around you in anticipation of you *asking* for what he wants to freely give you. If you have *believed* his truth that he desires you to not be a mistreated hostage, but instead that he dances around you with eager anticipation of you *asking* for his gifts, then consider this challenge: *ask* for whatever your heavenly Father promises. *Ask* for all God desires to give.

If you have not yet *accepted* the sacrifice of Jesus Christ as Savior and Lord—giving you access to the Father—and you have *believed* truth that God has presented to you, he wants you to *ask* for the very thing that the truth is presenting. What is the eternal issue that God desires us to *ask* him for? The most important *ask* at this point in your life is eternal life by *accepting* that Jesus Christ died for your sins to restore you to an eternal relationship with your heavenly Father.[87]

If you are a believer and God has *offered* something, he *offers* because he wants you to *ask*. Seek God about any areas of your life where you have *heard* and *believed* what he has *shared* with you and you have not pressed on to *ask*.[88] What is preventing you from *asking*? An example is *hearing* and *believing* about healing but not *asking* for your own healing. *Ask* for what God desires to *bless* you with as revealed in Scripture and by the Holy Spirit.

Promotion Beyond Ask

Promotion from God will not come until the *student celebrates* the growth and *worships* God as the changer. At this time of promotion, the *student* has *asked* for God's truth. This is a request to appropriate that truth for their personal growth. They are another *step* closer to being *transformed* by that truth.

God desires that the *student seek* him for the next *step* of growth, which is to *receive*. The *student* has *celebrated* the act of *asking*, and now God wants them to get the *revelation* of the need to *receive*. He will take action to promote that *revelation* in the *student* and will wait.

Reflections and Discussion

Please reflect on the questions presented in the section titled "Main Discussion Guide for the Student Process" on page 194. Additionally, the following questions focus on *ask*:

1. What happens when one *asks* Jesus to come into their lives to be Savior and Lord?

Receive

Assertion about Receive

To grow, we must deliberately *receive* and absorb what we have *asked* for. We must be a sponge for his truth. As new Christians, we *ask* Jesus to be Savior and Lord of our lives.[89] [90] *Receiving* Jesus as Savior grants us eternal life—salvation. Salvation affectively occurs when we get the spiritual awareness[91] that Jesus died to get us restored to fellowship with the Father. Salvation is an instantaneous event and, graphically said, is fire insurance—being saved from going to hell. The Lordship of Jesus is not an event; it is a process[92] that produces a lifestyle of yielding to God and honoring him in all that we *do*. To grow, we must *receive* and follow that process. If we do not follow *asking* with *receiving*, then we stagnate and cease to benefit from *ask*.

Consider asking for a drink of water, and then when it is delivered, we reject it. We get no benefit from it. The same is true with every gift of God that we *ask* for. We must *accept* what God *offers* us before we become the *receivers* of it. In Acts 19, Paul encountered disciples that were getting no benefit from the Holy Spirit after *believing*, because they did not even know to *receive* the Holy Spirit.[93] Right away, they *received* the Holy Spirit into their lives.[94]

When God says we will *receive* something, it means that he will *offer* that *blessing* to us to *accept* or to not accept. God *offers* when he instructs us to *receive* the gift of eternal life.[95] It would be different if that were a commandment that we were forced to obey, but God gave us the freedom to choose; and we have to exercise that free will. Man *accepts* when he says, "*I receive Jesus as my Savior and Lord.*" It is during *receiving* that one can assert that they know the truth that has set them free.[96]

God always has more <u>that</u> we can *receive,* and more <u>than</u> we can *receive.* In Joshua 13:1, after conquering lands for God for a long time, God spoke to Joshua and said, "*Joshua, you are an old man and still we have lands to conquer.*" We can serve our whole life, and God will still have more for us to *receive.* At that last moment when he says, "*Welcome home good and faithful servant,*"[97] we still have a wonderful gift to *receive* which is eternity with him!

The Journey of Receive

An essential part of growth during the journey of *receiving* is to recognize that all things come from God[98] and return to God. Recognizing that all things come from God and not from us is one significant difference between humility and pride.

The journey of *receiving* is recognizing that because we are forgiven, we are restored, and because we are restored, we are children of the living God.[99] Because we are children of the living God, we are heirs and have entitlements. God wants to pour out *blessings* on us.[100] Recognizing this truth helps us see that because of him we are worthy. *Receive* is a choice that is a required part of the process of growth.[101]

Miracles Associated with Receive

Any time we *receive* something from God,[102] it begins a *change* in us,[103] and that is a miracle. Every *blessing* is a gift from God, and every gift is a *blessing.* The first miracle that we can focus on is that we *receive* eternal life by faith.[104] Another miracle is that we *receive* the Holy Spirit by faith. Some new believers began *speaking* in tongues[105] when they *received* the Holy Spirit. Even when we *receive* discipline from our heavenly Father, we experience his love for us to draw us closer[106] to him,[107] and that too is a miracle.

The Journey That is Distant from Receive

When we are convinced that we have enough from God, we can stop being in the mindset of *receiving*.[108] God does not desire that we stop *receiving*; he wants us to *receive* always. If we get convinced by the enemy that we do not need God, he will have convinced us to stay distant from God. This distancing can manifest in us not being saved, being convinced that God does not exist or is not interested, or being a growth-starved Christian, unstable in many ways.

Blockages to Receive

Pride is the deceptive belief that we can accomplish tasks without God's help or leadership; it is a consideration that we can make it all on our own.[109] Pride is a chief blockage to *receiving,* because the very enemy of our lives has convinced us that we can do something on our own. Pride doubts God.[110] We have a crafty enemy, one who comes to steal, kill, and destroy.[111] His native tongue is deception,[112] and he deceives all he can into believing that they do not need God, his ways, or his Son. Satan's sin is pride, and he freely passes it out to all who will *accept* it.

The Journey toward Receive

God must cause this growth.[113] The *student* must get a *revelation* from God that they need to *receive* and then *desire* to *receive*. Prayer helps prepare hearts to *receive*. God would never *offer* anything to us, unless he wanted us to *receive* it. God tests us but never tempts us. He *offers* over and over but never demands that we *accept* what he is *offering*. He gives us commands and requirements to bring us into life,[114] but he does not demand obedience. He just desires obedience. He desires us to *accept* Jesus as Savior and Lord, but he does not demand it, because he permits us to choose.

Deuteronomy 30:19 says, "*This day I call heaven and earth as witnesses against you that I have set before you life and death, blessings and curses. Now choose life, so that you and your children may live.*" Notice the clauses "*Set before you*" and "*choose life*" indicate that God desires us to *accept* what he wants to give us, but we still have that choice.

God places his gifts before us to pick up. He does not say, "*I am just offering to be nice. You really have no choice. I demand you to take it!*" Instead he places his gift before us in our life, and we get to choose to pick it up or leave it there. Then he reminds us of the value of his gift, "*Choose life that you and your children may live.*"

The journey toward obedience of *receiving* starts with allowing trust to form in our hearts related to what God is doing. Trust is an integral part of *hearing* and *believing* and is a deepening of *believing*. The first journey through *believing* God's Word will not be nearly as deep as later journeys. God desires us to *believe* him at the deepest level. The deeper the level of *belief*, the more firm the trust. The more firm the trust, the easier it is to *receive*.

How Do We Start to Receive?

The *student* must *invite* this *step*. We must recognize that we are worthy to *receive* what the Father is *offering*. Isaiah 52:1–3 tells us that to begin healing, we must clothe ourselves with strength and then put on garments of splendor.[115] We must *receive* strength from the truth of God, and then clothe ourselves in his splendor by recognizing that we are children of God and are worthy of this rescuing and healing. As a child of God, you are worthy to *receive* what God wants you to *receive*.

Turn to God, and pray something like:

> *Father, I realize that I was missing your mercy and your gifts to me, when I would not receive what you wanted to give to me. Forgive me for having a hard heart. I ask for deeper faith, trust, and confidence in you to receive what you have to offer me. Thank you for free access to you Father, because of the sacrifice of Jesus Christ. I pray directly to you because of that sacrifice, and I thank you for fellowship with you in Jesus' name.*

Changing the Heart to Receive

Only God can *change* a heart. Pray for the heart that is resisting the call to *receive*. As we plant seeds, wait a time while tending and then anticipate harvest. Pray for God to make that heart into good soil to *receive* and produce fruit one hundred fold. It is the goodness of God that draws men to repentance,[116] and it is the goodness of God that draws all men to himself. The solution is to pray that God does his work in a person—or in you—to be allowed to *receive*.

The Challenge to Receive

The *student* must not only *permit* but also *embrace* and be *changed* by the *receiving step*. We *receive* his gifts and are awed, touched, and filled. *Receiving* opens the door to God *changing* us. When we *receive* a Word from God, he will begin to *teach* us to make that active in our lives. We will not see God's best in our lives without first *receiving* what he has given us. His Word does not return to him void but accomplishes what he sent it out to accomplish and the work to which it was sent.[117] His Word does indeed return to him, just never void. If you want in on what God is doing, you must *receive* what he is *blessing* you with.

Ask God if there is some area in your life that you have *heard*, *believed*, and *asked*; but for some reason, you've really not yet opened up to *receive*. Be encouraged right now to begin *receiving*. *Receive* eternal life by *accepting* that you cannot do the right thing enough times to make it to heaven on your own but only by *accepting* the sacrifice of Jesus Christ as your Savior. *Receive* from God the ability to learn to serve him in whatever way he is leading you to learn. *Receive* every *blessing* from your heavenly Father, because you are worthy—not because of who you are—but because of whose you are.

If you have *believed* the truth about the sacrifice of the blood of Jesus Christ[118] for your sins and you *asked* God for forgiveness,[119] your heavenly Father desires that you *receive* the truth that he forgave you and redeemed you and that you now have Jesus Christ as your personal Savior,[120] giving you eternal life[121] and a growing relationship with him. There is value in repeating this another way, by saying that if you have gone through the steps of *hearing*, *believing*, *asking*, and now *receiving* that Jesus Christ is your Savior, you have eternal life. *Receive* the gift that you now have access to the Father and that you have eternal life through the sacrifice of Jesus Christ.

This *receiving* is an intentional *embrace* of God's truth, knowing that he will begin the process of *changing* you from the inside out. You have *accepted* Jesus Christ as Savior, an event completed by God instantaneously. Now God desires for you to allow him to be not just Savior but Lord as well.

Lordship is not an event; it as a process of growth that begins after you *receive* him as Savior. You have new life inside you, because you have been born again[122] into the kingdom of God. God will continue to birth new life into you as you *permit* him. God will continue to encourage you to allow him to be, not just your Savior giving you eternal life, but also the Lord of your daily life on earth.[123] In other words, you were just born into eternity, and now God wants eternity to be born into you.

If you are a believer and God has been *teaching* you a nugget of truth to effect *change* and further his Lordship in your daily life, *receive* what he is sharing with you as something too wonderful to understand now, too awesome to comprehend, and too magnificent to decline. In the future, if not in the past, God will prove himself to you. He is trustworthy! He runs the universe[124] and energizes an uncountable number of galaxies, each with an uncountable number of atoms. Perhaps you can trust him to be giving you something for his glory and your joy.

Promotion beyond Receive

Promotion from God will not come, until the *student celebrates* the growth and *worships* God as the changer. At this time of promotion, the *student* has *received* God's truth. This is a glorious time, because they are *embracing* spiritual truth for personal growth. They are another *step* closer to being *transformed* by that truth.

God desires that the *student seek* him for the next *step* of growth, which is *doing*. The *student* has *celebrated receiving*, and now God wants them to get the *revelation* of the need to *do*. He will take action to promote that *revelation* in the *student* and will wait.

Reflections and Discussion

Please reflect on the questions presented in the section titled "Main Discussion Guide for the Student Process" on page 194.

Additionally, the following questions focus on the *step* of *receiving*:

1. What happens when one *receives* Jesus into their lives to be Savior and Lord?

2. Review Acts 19 and think about a time when God was trying to give you awareness of something that you did not want to *receive*. How were your actions more like the disciples in verse 1, or how were they more like the synagogue people in verse 8 and 9? What were the results of your choices?

3. Make a list of God's blessings upon you. Remember Philippians 4:8, and stop at twenty. If you laughed because twenty is too many, get with someone who has twenty or more and learn from them.

4. What miracles or wondrous events have you experienced, because you *received* what God was *offering* you?

Do

Assertion about Do

We let God *do* the Word through us. We honor what the scriptures call us to *do,* and we become *doers* of the Word.[125] We walk out the truth in obedience and faith.

Hearing alone is not enough, but it is the beginning of growth. When we *hear* truth and obey, we are *blessed.*[126] There is a *step* beyond *hearing;* we must obey; we must *do.*[127] *Doing* is as precise as it is vague, especially to the young believer. Because the truth is *received,* we can make an effort to *change* into what God wants, but we cannot *do* all the things requested in the Word. We have to let God *do* them through us. We must give him *permission* to accomplish this through us. If we attempt it ourselves, we are trying to accomplish God's will under our own power. Doing it under our own power is living under the law and making the law our target, and we cannot live by the law and satisfy God.[128] We must make our heavenly Father the target of our life and the *doing* will become a result of and fruit of our relationship with him.

Some believers live under bondage here. With good intentions and no further illumination, they live their lives by the law and stagnate, because they are performing the task from only the heart,[129] hoping to be *blessed* because they perform. Growth comes when they realize the freedom that God does his Word through them,[130] if they will just *permit* it to happen. Then, by the power of God, obedience is repeated for the rest of their lives and becomes their lifestyle.

An example might be praying for the sick. If the sick person is healed, who did it? Certainly we *accept* the answer that God healed the person.[131] God did his healing work through our faithful prayer.[132] It is the same for everything that God desires for us to accomplish. He wants to *do* it through us, whether it is a request to stop telling lies, to walk in sexual purity, to stop robbing, or to walk out a *role* in our life. It is not possible for a man to be a husband, unless God is a husband through him, and it is not possible for a woman to be a wife, unless God is a wife through her.

The Journey of Do

When we *do* the Word once, that obedience gives God joy, yet he has more growth planned for us. God in his infinite wisdom desires us to consistently engage in *doing* the Word and consistently walking out his truth in our lives, and then he begins to flow through us. *Doing,* motivated by God, goes from a one-time event to a permanent way of life. We are *transformed* by the renewing of our minds[133] and the conviction to be steadfastly *doing transforms* us from an event of *doing* into a lifestyle of *doing.* Steadfastly *doing* builds a road that leads to the next *step,* which is *care.*

Miracles Associated with Do

When Jesus walked the earth, he spoke and multitudes were convicted in their spirits and *believed.* They sought his truth and *received* what he had to *share* with them. When he was about to heal, he sometimes asked people to *do* things in faith. Sometimes they acted on their own without being asked by Jesus, because they were prompted by the Holy Spirit. They acted on what they had *received,* whether it was truth from heaven or healing from heaven. For some, the *do* was in the coming to him for healing. Their *do* was a response in faith; to *believe* him with no doubt. In Matthew 8:5–13,[134] the centurion had already matured through the steps of *hearing, believing, asking,* and *receiving*—outside of the story. He was acting on the truth of Christ that he had *received*. He was certain that God wanted to use Jesus to heal his servant. His *doing* was not only in coming but in confessing his awareness of the truth that Jesus could heal without visiting the sick personally.

The Journey That is Distant from Do

Many of us know of people who talk the talk but are not walking the walk: those who talk of Jesus but do not live as if they have been *transformed* by the renewing of their minds and those who talk at length about God but are really short on him. We are to judge no man but to judge all things by the Spirit.[135] Judgment is reserved for God, yet we are called to perceive the presence of the Spirit in all things.[136] You will know them by the fruit of their lives.[137]

There are those who do not effectively walk out the Word. They do not appear to be growing after *receiving* truth. They do not appear to recognize that they are rocky soil. Spiritually, they influence very little, because rocky soil does not sharpen rocky soil.[138] Rocky soil is not ready for the seed of truth, because it does not contain the nutrients required to promote growth.

An example of being distant from *doing* is in Genesis 4:4-8.[139] Cain had been doing wrong in God's eyes, and God did not look upon him with favor. Instead of being humble and *seeking* God's answer, Cain got angry about being out of favor with God. God tells him that to earn favor, he must do right. Sin wanted to overtake Cain, but God wanted him to master it and do what was right. Perhaps you know someone who has done something wrong and the enemy gets them to be angry at God instead of repenting and *seeking* to *do* things God's way. In verse 8, Cain killed Abel, because he was defiantly distant from *doing*—one of the first examples of the truth that there is a way that seems right to a man but its end is death.[140]

Blockages to Do

A heart that does not *receive* what God has spoken into their lives has a blockage to *doing*. This hardened heart has little recognition of conviction, little compulsion to obey, and little interest in following.

Until *receiving* happens, the process remains incomplete, growth is stagnant, and true freedom is not realized. Until the *student receives* that they are children of the most-high God and are entitled to the all of the benefits of that position, they are not inclined to act on that truth.

If a *student* has *received* but is not *doing*, it may be that they do not see the value of *doing*. They may be brokenhearted, out of faith, and tired of *operating* on their own. God will want to have them see his safety so that they may recognize the value of *doing*.

The Journey toward Do

God must cause this growth. The *student* must get a *revelation* from God that they need to *do* and then *desire* to *do*. Prayer helps prepare hearts to *do*. God draws us to this growth with his love.[141] God is the tiller of our lives and hearts.[142] It is by his efforts that we are *transformed* from rocky soil to fertile ground. Observe mountains to understand that God is the tiller. Can man level a mountain range and turn it into plains of fertile soil, or can a field of granite produce corn with stalks every few inches? God has to work on the heart of granite. Only he can turn granite into fertile soil. Only he can turn hard hearts into hard workers with soft hearts.

How Do We Start to Do?

The *student* must *invite* this *step*. They must want to walk out the truth that sets them free.[143] When their heart is convicted and motivated to be obedient to the Word that has been *received*, they may be obedient and *do* something in faith the first time. An example might be a prayer that sounds like,

> *Okay, God, I understand that even though I do not feel like forgiving this person, you know what is good for me and you have shown me that Satan will have a stronghold in my emotions until I forgive. I am convinced by your truth that when I forgive, Satan will lose his hold on me in that area. Since I am aware of that now, I no longer want to allow Satan to steal any victory in my life that I could have with you. I will forgive as you ask me to, God. I forgive completely and release bitterness. I surrender to you. I put all of the garbage from*

that stronghold into my cupped hands, and I reach up to you and offer these things to you. I let go of them and dump them into your outstretched hands. Thank you for taking these hurts and handling the bitter lies of the enemy. Thank you that by me forgiving this act against me, I forgive the vessel of the action because that vessel belongs to you.

This prayer is righteous,[144] because it is living out the *step* of *doing*. This prayer walks out, *"Love others as yourself."*[145] This prayer follows God's example, because he forgives us and we become examples of Christ.[146] This prayer breaks strongholds in lives and sets the one praying into freedom instead of bondage. *Doing* puts us on a road of obedience that sets us free.[147]

Changing the Heart to Do

To *change* the heart to *do* mode, the *student* has to see value in *doing*. It helps to have others around who sharpen and call them up higher and higher. Proverbs 27:17 says, *"As iron sharpens iron, so one man sharpens another."* The *student* sees others *doing* and hears their testimony.[148] They see *changed* lives by seeing those examples, and by an act of grace from God, begin to see value in *doing*.

The Challenge to Do

The *student* must not only *permit* but also *embrace* and be *changed* by the *doing step*. Are you walking out his Word in your life every moment that you are not asleep? Is your life as you *desire* it to be? Is it as God desires it to be? Are you being the best that you can be in God's calling? Are you *asking* for and *seeking* God's truth in your life? When you *hear* truth from God's Word, are you *seeking* clarification from God and his counsel about how to integrate that into your spirit, your thinking, and your life, so you can *do* that Word?[149]

Ask God to make you aware of any area of your life where you have *heard*, *believed*, *asked*, and even *received*, but are in a struggle to *do* the Word that he desires. What might be preventing you from *doing*? Forgiveness is an example: we are taught about forgiveness and we obediently forgive someone, yet when we are around the one we forgave, we can barely *do* the Word. We can hardly walk out that forgiveness. The enemy tempts us to retaliate in some way. Are you having trouble with *doing?*

If you have recently *received* Jesus Christ as Savior, your heavenly Father desires that you *do* what his Word is *teaching* you.[150] This is the initial *step* of allowing him to be Lord in your life. This is an essential part of growth and maturity. By being a *doer* and not just a *hearer* only, you will find that God's ways are always better.[151] Repentance[152] is a part of this: to turn from ways that are not authored by him and to begin to walk his path.[153] Truth promises us in Acts 2:38 that repentance and baptism are essential to get the *offer* of the gift of the Holy Spirit. The Holy Spirit is essential to the next *step* of growth. The *step* of *doing* is where God *teaches* us that his ways accomplish his purpose and they are always better than our ways. Our ways always lead to death not life.

If you are a believer and God has been *teaching* you to walk out his Word and walk in holiness, he wants you to *do* the Word. *Seek* out ways to *do* God's Word and how to walk out the truth. *Seek* to allow God to convict you of his truth, and allow God to *do* his Word through you. First, he will allow his truth to work *in* you, until you are *transformed* in *care* mode. He will then allow his truth to work *through* you as you go through *show*. In *show* mode others will know by silent example that he is Lord in your life. Let God *do* the Word through you. *Do* what the scriptures say, and become a *doer* of God's Word.

Promotion beyond Do

Promotion from God will not come until the *student celebrates* the growth and *worships* God as the changer. At the time of promotion, the *student* is *doing* what God's truth is calling them to *do*. During this *step,* the *student* has learned that *doing* things God's way produces his results, and his results are best. They are another *step* closer to being *transformed* by the renewing of their minds.

God desires that the *student seek* him for the next *step* of growth, which is *care*. The *student* has *celebrated do*, and now God wants them to get the *revelation* of the need to *care*. God wants to cultivate the *student* from just *doing* the Word and walking in rigid obedience to seeing incalculable value in his truth and *caring* for it, according to its spiritual value. He will take action to promote that *revelation* in the *student* and will wait.

Reflections and Discussion

Please reflect on the questions presented in the section titled "Main Discussion Guide for the Student Process" on page 194. Additionally, the following questions focus on *do*:

1. Why is it important in your life to *do* things God's way?

2. Can you be a *doer* of the Word, strictly following God's plans and not be a legalist? What is the difference between being a *doer* of the Word as a legalist and being a *doer* of the Word as one set free?

3. Reflect on Proverbs 14:12 and Psalm 127:1, and consider what you are *doing* by God's direction. What are you *doing* that is not by God's direction?

4. What does it look like in your daily life to be a *doer* of the Word?

5. What does it mean to you that it is not possible for a man/woman to be a husband/wife, unless God is husband/wife through them?

6. What kind of strongholds had to be broken in your life for you to become a consistent *doer* of the Word?

Care

Assertion about Care

This is a time when we *care* for God's Word that we have been given. We are *changed* by his truth.[154] His Word is truth. This is a time of tending that truth. The Word begins to *change* us on the inside. We allow it to happen, so we can grow according to God's plan.[155] We must do what we can to fan the flame, feed the fire, and tend the truth.[156] It is a time when we openly, intentionally, and gratefully allow Jesus to become Lord in our lives, not just as our Savior. Salvation is instantaneous, and Lordship is a process. We are *transformed* into his likeness by truth. He sent his Word forth to accomplish this at creation.

Care mode is the significant *step* where we allow Jesus to be Lord in our lives. During this *step*, we learn that we cannot make Jesus Lord of our lives by force of action or force of will. We learn that all we can do is tend to our heart, *seeking* to be a fertile heart that requests truth to reign in us. During this *step*, we learn that we can make God Lord in our lives by allowing him to *change* our thinking. Our massive effort is limited to *caretaking* his work in our hearts and to being ready and willing to allow him to do anything he needs to do to cleanse our heart and life.

During this *step,* we let go of the untruth and corruption that the enemy had convinced us to hold on to. This *step* includes allowing

God to redeem brokenness and wounding in our lives and taking *care* to allow him to *transform* our beliefs and actions. This is a time of substantial spiritual growth. There are many Christians in the world that either never enter or are stuck in this *step*, as evidenced by the fruit of their lives and in their witness. God is waiting for their *permission* before he will *change* them.

The Journey of Care

This is a miraculous journey to complete. It is similar to maturing from a child to an adult, from being self-centered to being focused on others, and from being foolish to being wise. Only God knows the way he works this out. Once we were blind, but now we see.[157] Jesus *shares* a parable in Matthew 13:44 and presents heaven as treasure in a field.[158] A *student* not in the step of *care* would see the jewel in the field and not perceive any value. But a *student* showing diligence to *do* what God has revealed to them *transforms* from the obedient do-slave into one recognizing incalculable value in the Word that has been planted in them.

In this subtle and powerful shift of thought and *revelation*, one turns from just being a do-robot and *doing* the truth in obedience into an ecstatic farmer/rancher erecting God-fences to keep the enemy out and allow the truth to grow.[159] An effort is made to be sure the truth is planted deeply, so it produces strong roots.[160] The immense value of the truth that *transforms* begins to be perceived. The *student* now knows that great value is achieved from allowing God to till this soil and then protecting that growing truth.[161] This protection and *care* happens by putting on a shield of faith—a shield of *believing* truth whose fruit has not yet been seen.[162] Like finding the jewel in the field, the *student* is willing to sell all that is owned to acquire and retain and *care* for just that one gem of truth.[163] The absolute beauty of God is that as soon as we are willing to sell all that we own to acquire and protect the truth, the transaction is complete, we still have all that we owned, and now we have even more, because we have added God's solid truth to our lives.

Miracles Associated with Care

Every life is a miracle after it has been *transformed* by *caretaking* the planted Word. There has been a miracle associated with *caretaking* when someone *seeks* testimony from the *student* noting, *"You are not the same. I see a different you. What happened inside of you?"* When we testify before a group about what God has done in us, a miracle is revealed associated with *caring*. It is a miracle, because we have been durative in our protection of God's Word in us.

Adam and Eve were put in the Garden of Eden to be *caretakers*.[164] God gave them things to protect and nurture. He does the same thing with us, as he gives us truth that is intended to *transform* us. We are *transformed* by the renewing of our minds. The *transformation* is not automatic; it is a result of *accepting* truth and being good soil to produce one-hundred-fold fruit from that truth[165]—it is a result of us being in *care* mode and *caretaking* truth.

The Lordship of Jesus is *accepted* and sought during this *step* of growth. God constantly and consistently performs his internal miracles here. Our *role* is to diligently protect, and if necessary, fearfully work to ensure that we are good soil to allow truth to grow.[166] Like soil, we cannot force the seed of truth to grow; we can only put forth effort to be good soil, *accept* truth in faith, and allow it to grow.[167] Consider the potter and the clay.[168] The clay may think it is doing all of the work, because it is bending and moving, but the *change* is caused by the potter, not the clay. The clay need only give *permission* for the *change*. Allowing him to be Lord in us requires that we do nothing except allow him to *transform* us and respond to that truth, protect it, tend it, *embrace* it, and *invite* more truth. We cannot accomplish this without him *doing* it, and he will not *do* it without our *permission*.

The Journey That is Distant from Care

The enemy, who comes to destroy,[169] uses his agents to stomp through some lives, stirring up trouble and every vile and disgusting thing and thought.[170] Similar to the weed-filled ground in the Parable of the Sower, the enemy stirs up life issues that keep some so busy that they do not take time to either meditate on the truth or medicate with the truth. They do not plant truth deeply, and because of this, they find themselves wondering why the occasional *doing* of the Word does not work for them.

The truth is that stopping at just *doing* the Word will starve the growth of anyone. Growth will starve, if we do not mature into *caretaking* of that Word and be *transformed* by the renewing of the mind. It is good when the *student* is in *do*-mode, because the *student* is walking the way of God and obediently following commands, but God desires more: he desires their growth.

Maturing to the realization that truth must be guarded and protected immerses the *student* in the vitally important *step* of *care*. This *caretaking step* will call them upwards to protect the truth that *transforms*, and grows into a walk of holiness. If the *student* is caught up in the issues of this world, attending to only them, and not what is important to God, they can get caught in the trap of just an occasional *do*, hoping to please God with their performance. This *student* is not focused on growth caused by saturation in truth. This *student* may not become *transformed*. Suffering from the lack of role models, this *student* is content to allow Jesus to be just Savior and not Lord.

This is where many growth-starved Christians are stuck, and where, for example, we can find the drunken Christian in a bar with the words of God's love sloshing out of their mouth, wondering why no one is being drawn towards the God they supposedly serve. Another troubled *student* might be serving in the church in some capacity yet still be in bondage in some area of life that God has spoken to him about, such as alcohol, drugs, or inappropriate sexual activity. God desires them to be willing to grow and allow him to *change* them, yet the enemy has them so wrapped up in pleasures that they are not focused on *change* and growth. They can perform in church,[171] but they will not be as an *affective* vessel while dragging their sin along with them.

God is aware of their issue and may not promote them, because promotion will expose others to—and possibly infect others with—their unrefined activities.[172] The *student* will have trouble progressing, because the value of the treasure of God's gift has not been fully perceived.[173]

Blockages to Care

We cannot be *caretakers of* the Word when we have not been *doing* the Word. We must *do* the Word. The Word cannot be planted deeply in our heart if it is not being walked out on the surface of our lives. If someone is not willing to *do* the Word, they will not arrive at the *step* of *caring* to be able to be *caretakers of* that truth.

Because of what he himself has done in some lives, the enemy has caused some to be filled with anger. It is difficult to *care* for truth from God if we are angry at God. With cunning imposed only by someone whose native tongue is deception,[174] Satan never brings up his own name. Instead he points to God, our loving Father, and convinces us that the turmoil he has stirred up was caused by God. Satan gets his victory, when we believe him and not honor God and hold a grudge against God, as if he really did inflict this damage upon us. Understand the source of the turmoil. Three words we will never hear Satan say on this side of eternity are, *"It was me."* When his lie is recognized, then the deceiver of the brethren can be addressed. If there is a blockage to *caring*, look for the enemy, bring his deception out into the light, and turn to God for forgiveness, instant *acceptance*, and *revelation* of the truth.

If you have ever taught a child to ride a bike, you will recall that it is not the falls that we carry forward in memory but just the success of riding. It is the *celebration* of the victory of balance. It is the *celebration* of learning, not the punishment for failures. It is the joy of watching the new rider delicately wobble away on their own, as they finally learn that art of steering and peddling to progress forward. The enemy of our lives wants us to focus on failures, but God wants to focus on successes.

God is more concerned about our *believing* him than about punishing us for not *believing*. It is about the "Ah, ha" moments not the "Oh, no" moments. If God wants us to focus on whatever is pure, lovely, admirable, true, noble, or right and to search (*seek* out and hunt for) anything excellent or praiseworthy,[175] how much more does God think that way about us? God focuses on anything in our lives that is excellent or praiseworthy, because it is his nature! If someone has stumbled and fallen, the enemy will lie to them and cause them to focus on the fall, but God is next to them lovingly calling out to *care* for the truth with, *"Come on! Forget the fall! I have so much more for you! Let's try again! We have places to go! Let me show you again how to ride this bicycle! Let's go, go, go! You can do it!"*

The Journey toward Care

God must cause this growth. The *student* must get a *revelation* from God that they need to *care* and then *desire* to *care*. Prayer helps prepare hearts to *care*. The *"Hmmm"* moment arrives when first we obey and see results. The *"Ah, ha"* moment certainly arrives when we see the fruit of repetition blooming. The realization that the Word of truth inside of us is precious births a *desire* to protect and defend, to tend, and nurture—to *caretake*.

How Do We Start to Care?

The *student* must *invite* this *step and* then jealously guard the truth within them. Walk by the power of God, and live like he desires you to live. You *can* do all things with the strength of God.[176] God will not call you to do something that he will not *empower* you to complete.[177] Make the choice to be a *doer* over and over and over again—until it becomes a way of life and a *change* of perspective is accomplished in the heart.[178] Confronted with the old way of *doing* things and God's way, choose God's way, not because God's way is fully understood, but because it is understood that the Father of the universe has a plan and pattern for living that works every time. His Word does not return to him void but accomplishes that which it was sent forth to accomplish.[179] The Psalms and Proverbs are replete with admonishments to *care* for knowledge, wisdom, and understanding. A good example is Psalm 119:34, *"Give me understanding, and I will keep your law and obey it with all my heart."*

Changing the Heart to Care

This is where the majority of growth-starved Christians are stuck. What does it take to move a heart to go beyond just being a *doer* and be completely *transformed* by the renewing of their minds?

What does it take to get us to be as radically different from the world as God desires? What does it take to allow us to see that the life we live without the fullness of God is a shallow empty shell? God has much more to give and desires to draw us back to him.

Pain is a big motivator: pain of past failure, present failure, or future failure and pain of missing out on the best that God has to *offer*. Is there pain? Look for the enemy of our lives to find the source of the pain. Are we *doing* what God desires us to *do* and not being durative? Are we pliable clay in the potter's hands? Do we see value in God's way? Do we have a soft heart?

Compare the way of the world and the way of God to determine if we are handling an event the way God desires us to handle it. At this point in our walk, we are already being a *doer*. Is our faith shallow, or is it a deep flowing river? Is the truth *changing* us? Are we being *changed* by being a *doer* over and over again? Is there passion to *care* for the jewel we have discovered? Allow God to *change* your heart, give him *permission* to *transform* your thinking, and conform it to his. He is the one who created the universe and does not change;[180] He says to us, "*Child, you and I are not compatible,*[181] *and I don't change.*"[182] Allow God to *change* you.

The Challenge to Care

The *student* must not only *permit* but also *embrace* and be *changed* by the *caretaking step*. We *care* for what God has given us, attend to the details of daily living in his truth, and obtain redemption of brokenness and wounding in our own lives. This will manifest as *change*. We are *transformed* by the renewing of our minds.[183] This is where the rubber meets the road. This is where we walk out the process of allowing Jesus to be Lord in our lives.

If *doing* can be referenced as intentional obedience, then *caretaking* can be referenced as intentional tending. Both are acts of free will, yet the *doing* of the Word is not nearly as life *changing* as the intentional tending of truth. During this time of *caretaking*, we are doing nothing to make it happen, except allowing God to *change* us completely: to allow the truth to *transform* our core thinking and core model of behavior. We are indeed *transformed* by the renewing of our minds. Make the intentional choice to *ask* God to *change* you to *care* mode, to allow you to see the value in jealously guarding that truth within you, and to allow his *change* in you.

If you have recently *accepted* Jesus Christ as Savior and Lord and have been diligently walking out his Word in your life, your heavenly Father desires that you make the special effort to tend and *care* for his truth planted in you. The *caretaking step* is a guarding time, and the truth we guard and *caretake* will *change* us from the inside out.

During our growth in this *step*, much of what we used to think was cool, neat, and wise will become as useless as dust. All we can do is put forth effort to ensure that we are good soil that allows the seed to grow. When the seed of a tree is planted in fertile soil, we tend, protect, and watch, waiting for the growth to produce fruit. When God plants truth in us and we enter *care*, our efforts in the *change* are limited to tending, protecting, and watching, perhaps for years, and then we can rejoice about what he has grown in us.

It is important to note that we are the fertile soil; we are not the seed. The seed will grow by God's design, if we are fertile. Only God can cause the seed to grow, so our effort in this *caretaking step* is doing nothing, except allowing God to grow the seed of truth in us. *Embrace* the *caretaking step* as a new Christian and wait with eager anticipation for the growth that God has for you. You may not be able to understand it on this side of the growth process,[184] but on the other side, you will be in wonder and awe, boasting only on him[185] and what he has done in you.

If you are a believer and God has been *teaching* you to walk out his Word and walk in holiness, he wants you to enter this *caretaking step* with eager anticipation. Wait patiently[186] on the Lord to cause this growth and complete his *transformation* of you from the inside out. Growth will be evident it its time. Keep trusting the Lord and intentionally tending the truth. Continue to guard your heart and motives to ensure that you are good soil which will allow you to produce fruit one hundred fold. Ask God to make you aware of any area of your life where you have *heard, believed, asked, received,* and are even *doing* the Word and are in a time of *care* to let the Word *transform* your mind and actions.

You might feel like you are on a back burner during this time. Go to God to *seek* answers. Are you stuck or just growing slower than you prefer to grow? Where is the enemy of your soul and deceiver of the believers, and what is he doing that is impacting your life during this *step*? What might be a stumbling block here? Are you being *transformed*, or are you preoccupied with the cares of the world? Are you *embracing* this *transformation* and pressing on to maturity or has the deceiver convinced you to do other things?

Promotion beyond Care

Promotion from God will not come until the *student celebrates* the growth and *worships* God as the changer. At this time of promotion, the *student* is *caring* for God's truth. During this *step*, the *student* has learned that it is intensely important for their personal life to erect God fences around his truth, to protect that truth, and to tend it—all to allow it to grow to produce good fruit one hundred fold. They are now being *transformed* by the renewing of their minds. By the power of God, their *transformation shows* by silent example.

God desires that the *student seek* him for the next *step* of growth, which is *show*. The *student* has *celebrated care*, and now God wants them to get the *revelation* of the need to *show*. He will take action to promote that *revelation* in the *student* and will wait.

Reflections and Discussion

Please reflect on the questions presented in the section titled "Main Discussion Guide for the Student Process" on page 194.
Additionally, the following questions focus on *care*:

1. In your effort of *caretaking* truth and being *changed*, how much *change* was from God and how much was from you (Read Psalm 127:1)?

2. How much *change* in your thinking happened without your *permission*?

Show

Assertion about Show

This is first and foremost a silent *show* of the fruit of the Spirit,[187] which is love, joy, peace, patience, kindness, goodness, faithfulness, gentleness, and self-control. The *show* is for the Father of life,[188] but in God's time others will see it too. This is where God *empowers* us. This *step* cannot occur without the power of the Holy Spirit.

The fruit of this maturing is allowing the Lordship of Jesus to be displayed in your life; it is living out and *operating* in the fruit of the Spirit.[189] We *show* the Father that Jesus is Lord in our lives by our actions alone and others see too.[190] This is not a ministry action but a lifestyle of *showing* to God and man.[191] The Bible indicates that we can appear before God and church leadership to *show* ourselves approved. Others will notice the *change* because he will make it obvious.[192]

During this *step,* God fills us with the Holy Spirit, and we begin to *show* proof. God's gifts for service become more evident. We see his gifts and callings in us and continue to let him develop and mature the gifts that he put in us to serve him. When we allow our lives to be controlled by the movement of the Holy Spirit, we *operate* in humble kingdom boldness.

The Journey of Show

Pride can be defined as us feeling like we can *do* things by ourselves. Humility can be defined as recognizing that all things come from God. *Showing* is a walking out of humility. *Showing* can only come from that which is inside, when everything else can easily be flesh boasting in pride.[193] We have allowed ourselves to be *transformed* by the renewing of our minds, and we are different from the inside out.[194]

This is where the wisdom of God begins to be evident and where we have that unsolicited urge to volunteer to help someone, not because they are worthy or that we are trying to prove a point, but our agenda is an outpouring of truth and love. Like gravity pulls water down a river, so the truth pulls us to respond, as God would have us respond. The temper that used to flare up is rarely seen, and the habits, which used to have a stronghold on our lives, lose root and float away allowing God to flow through us. We are clean vessels.[195] Christians whom we encounter notice and appreciate Jesus working through us. They are not afraid to tell us about the *changes* they notice. Some people like how God comes through us so much that they tend to hang around us frequently, because they *see* what God is *showing*: himself in us. We are proud, not of ourselves, but proud of what God has done *in* us and finally *through* us.[196] James 3:13 comes to life in our understanding without the need for interpretation, because we realize that it is a statement of the life we now live, as we read, *"Let him show it by his good life, by deeds done in the humility that comes from wisdom."* We openly give honor and praise to God for the *changes* we know are inside, and others confirm it as well. Wisdom has found a home in us, and pride no longer has an invitation.[197]

Miracles Associated with Show

The Spirit of truth *empowers* us to *show*. In the four gospels, the many miracles of God through Jesus Christ were the *showing step* before he spoke. In Acts, after the disciples were *empowered* by the Holy Spirit in baptism, miracles began to occur. Anytime the Holy Spirit of God is in us, he sets the stage for miracles both small and large. It is in this part of growth where others are most likely to notice a quiet display of gentleness. Those that knew us before cannot deny the *change*, and those who recently met us are moved by the God they see shining through us. It is the goodness of God that draws men to repentance.[198] These efforts by God prepare others to *hear*, as he tills the rocks and turns them into good soil. Miracles in the New Testament were not salvation experiences for the observer, but the observer experienced something undeniable in the flesh and in spiritual perception, something which opened their eyes, ears, and hearts to the thought that perhaps the kingdom of God was near. This *show* produces a tilling of the soil and prepares others to *believe*.

The Journey That is Distant from Show

When a *student* has passed through *caretaking* and is distant from *showing*, most likely the enemy is up to something or has accomplished some harm in their life. *Showing* is a natural progression of the *change* of *caretaking* the truth inside us. Emotional harm comes to mind, including bitterness, rage, anger, and conflict. These emotions need to be dealt with by a trusted counselor or trained *servant* in the church. This may be a fruitful effort, because they may be able to clarify to the *student* where and why they are not progressing.

Blockages to Show

When one gets to this stage of growth in godliness, there has already been growth through *hear, believe, ask, receive, do,* and *care*. The Word has been working in us and *changing* us. There are perhaps other reasons that there would be blockage to *showing*, yet what seems most clear is a spirit of confusion. God *empowers* us, yet with all that the enemy has done in our lives—or perhaps what we have been taught—we still cling to the old way and exhibit no evidence of *change* in our lives or hearts.

Some have believed the toxic lie that the enemy of our lives has poured into us and into our influencing family, culture, and/or government. The lie has mistakenly affirmed that Christianity is a private thing. Many of us have heard someone say, *"My faith is a very private thing.*" Where did Jesus order us to keep faith quiet or keep it to ourselves? Jesus ordered the healed not to reveal who he was, because it was not yet time to *share* that news.[199] He was fulfilling prophecy. Later he told us to let our light shine before men.[200] Perhaps they don't know or perceive that truth from James 3:13, "*I will show you my faith by what I do.*"

The Journey towards Show

God must cause this growth. The *student* must get a *revelation* from God that they need to *show* and then *desire* to *show*. Prayer helps prepare hearts to *show*. Getting a vision of a higher calling and understanding its value can be a highly motivating experience. We are *transformed* and motivated by perceiving and *believing* that God desires to use us more and more, until we are an effective vessel for his glory.

A perspective that provides a more clear understanding is the realization that there are no great men and women of God, only men and women of a great God. God is no respecter of persons.[201] He assigns some certain roles—some pastor large churches and some sweep floors. All serve God, and all can *show* by silent example that he is Lord in their lives. The importance is not in the *role*; the importance is in walking out the *role* that God has laid upon us.[202] Is his Lordship evident, as we walk out our *role*? Are we faithful in little? If so, God indicates that he will trust us with more until more becomes much. Promotion to another *role* may or may not come; nevertheless, our *role* and our humble *desire* will be that God is given glory for what he is doing in us and through us.

How Do We Start to Show?

The *student* must *invite* this *step* and want to *show*. Like a fullnight's sleep shows on a rested face, the result of *care* becomes clear, and from that perspective, *show* is automatic. These evidences are a natural byproduct of a life *changed* by the Lordship of Jesus Christ. For example, the focus *changes* from the maturing thought of, "*I must not condemn others today,*" to a natural-flowing ponder and a never-ceasing, silent interaction with God, *seeking* to be a clear conduit, allowing others to see the Father and give praise to the King. The *change* is a shift from focusing on living by the law of "do not do your sin that you've been guilty of," to the role of the *servant* that leaves the rigidity of obeying the law behind like filthy rags and *embraces* a lifestyle of looking to the Father for the slightest hint of an opportunity to *bless* others and to perhaps be a vessel to offer a cup of water to a thirsty soul. Living a godly life is a byproduct of our relationship with God. It is the fruit of a higher call instead of a mandate to perform the law.

Common examples might be the deliverance from bondage that many experience, as they give their lives to God. One day, they notice that some of those bad habits that they used to struggle with have been left behind, and they may not even remember when the urgings, cravings, or obsessions ceased. Others approach the *student* and remark that they notice a *change*. The mature response gives God credit for the *transformation*.

At the high end of *change*—perhaps where our loving Lord would desire most of us to be—is the effecting of miracles, just to give glory to him and give joy to either ourselves or others. This is the place where we are so wonderfully and radically *transformed* that we live in expectancy of God using us to get the attention of others by whatever means *glorifies* him the most. Our highest *desire* is to be a clean vessel, whether the service is sweeping the floor or raising the dead. As long as the action serves and is in response to the Father of life, our joy is full.

Changing the Heart to Show

We may witness a higher walk by others who are in a more mature walk than we are. They call us up, encourage us to walk out the walk, and live out the *role*, which God has assigned us. Truth from Proverbs 27:17 says, *"As iron sharpens iron, so one man sharpens another."* How wondrously this passage describes the situation when humble Christians eagerly *embrace* growth.

The Challenge to Show

The *student* must not only *permit* but also *embrace* and be *changed* by the *showing step*. We *show* others that Jesus is Lord in our lives by our actions alone. Is the fruit of the Spirit *showing* in your life? Ask God if there is some area of your life where you have *heard, believed, asked, received,* are *doing,* and *caring,* but the fruit is not *showing* fully. How does he desire to increase your *showing* of him? For example consider issues, such as: smoking, drinking, gluttony, language, relationship behaviors, attitudes, thoughts, and faithfulness. Consider what you are doing when no one sees you and when you think no one will know.

Showing builds foundations, not for God, but for us. Maturity in the *step* of *showing* is meant to embolden. Consider the first time we use a complex formula in a mathematical-training exercise; the homework effort is intense and requires focus and repetition to see the value in the formula. The educational system provides problems for us to repeat just to train our minds. On the other side of the many training examples, we have a more firm idea of the usefulness of the exercises and the value of the formula. Given the right training, we can *show* that we know the formula by the way we casually and confidently solve a problem using the formula. Similarly, God will expose us to multiple examples as we walk out our *role* to cause us to learn the value of his way of doing things. We will see that his ways work, as evidenced by the fruit, and we will become bolder to do things his way.

God's way is always best. At first, we may not understand this absolute spiritual truth, but as we do things his way, we see over and over again that allowing him to be complete Lord over every facet of our lives produces one-hundred-fold fruit.[203] We now see and can *share* with multiple testimonies that there is a safe and wonderful truth to the scripture, that says in Proverbs 14:12, "*There is a way that seems right to a man, but in the end it leads to death.*" God puts before us life and death and asks us to choose life.[204] Choose his way; choose life. Your choice will *show* silently and profoundly.

We *operate* in maturity, we are humbly driven by his power, we are surrounded in amazement, we are in awe by evidences of his presence, and we see miracles and good fruit. The twenty-four elders are in awe and *worship* for eternity,[205] so it is acceptable to be amazed and awed by what he does through us. When we are *transformed* into his maturity and are surrounded by the "whatevers" of

Philippians 4:8.[206] We focus on only the good coming from God and through others, allowing our minds to be conduits of God's love by focusing on what is pure, lovely, admirable, true, noble, right, excellent, or praiseworthy. Living in those "whatevers" breeds followers, calls *seekers*, attracts the hurting, and motivates the lukewarm. This lifestyle displays the goodness of God, and it is the goodness of God that draws men to repentance.

If you have recently *accepted* Jesus Christ as Savior and Lord and have been diligently walking out his Word in your life, your heavenly Father desires that you *show* evidence of a *changed* life. This is a natural progression of maturity through guarding the truth and jealously protecting it in your life. This is not you *showing* off for man[207] but living to please God, because you are sure that what he has taught you is actually the most excellent way. Let it *show*! God wants you to be excited about *showing* off to him, and he is excited too. He is excited about your growth and your future. Your excitement can easily sound like, "*Father, I am so excited about what you are doing in me. Thank you! I see such a change recently, and I am so awed and humbled by what you have done. I think that my friends notice too, but even if they do not, I am glad that you notice.*"

If you are a believer and God has been *teaching* you to walk out his Word and to walk in holiness, he wants you to enter this *step* of *showing*. He wants you to exhibit to him that you are producing fruit one hundred fold and that you will diligently walk his way, because it is now part of the core of who he has made you. God has not cultivated you to this point to just retire you; he has good things planned. Promotion will come, because he has work for you to do. This *step* is just to *show* that his truth is producing excellent fruit in you. Keep guarding and tilling his *teaching*, and it will *show*. Feel free and *invited* to praise him and thank him for what he has done in you and what he will do through you, when the right time comes. An example might be that the focus of your heart has *changed* about those nearest to you; you and others notice that you live to *show* the peace and glory of God in your interactions with them. You live to bring God praise and *show* him to others.

Promotion beyond Show

Promotion from God will not come until the *student celebrates* the growth and *worships* God as the changer. At this time of promotion, the *student* is *showing* that God has *changed* them. During this *step*, the *student* has learned that they cannot take credit for the *change*, and they give God the *glory* for this *transformation*. The *transformation*, which renewed their minds, has produced a fruit that is obvious to others.

God desires that the *student seek* him for the next *step* of growth, which is *sharing*. The *student* has *celebrated showing*, and now God wants them to get the *revelation* of the need to *share*. God desires to move the *student* from *showing* by silent example into openly *sharing* that he has *changed* them and what he has taught them. He will take action to promote that *revelation* in the *student* and will wait.

Reflections and Discussion

Please reflect on the questions presented in the section titled "Main Discussion Guide for the Student Process" on page 194. Additionally, the following questions focus on *show*:

1. List the ways you are *showing* the *transformation* of God in your life. What does it look like in your daily life to *show* that your heavenly Father is your Lord?

2. What does a silent *show* of God look like when it is flowing through your life and what effect does that have on both believers and non-believers?

3. What does it mean to you that pride no longer has a home in you?

4. What is your understanding of the difference between pride and humility?

5. What lifestyle did you or will you leave behind as filthy rags when God begins to *show* through you?

Share

Assertion about Share

We *share* what God has taught us. We *share* the message of Christ and the love of God with others, as we are sent by the Holy Spirit.[208] This is ministry that responds to and serves God.[209] We operate in the gifts that God has given us and matured in us. This is being so filled with his truth and giftedness that there is an intentional effort, backed by a call of God to influence and serve others in his name. In power and authority, we stand against deception when we are attacked by it.[210] We *share* the message of Christ and the love of God with others, as we are sent by the Holy Spirit. This is the cup of water. This is using your gifts. This is a humble honor.[211] This is humble power.[212] The effort includes missions, evangelism, and other gifts of service.[213]

It is inappropriate for ministries to call one to serve unless God has developed the *student* to this *step*. The *student* would be immature and ineffective. God would not call a one-week-old Christian to lead an in-depth Bible study to reveal his deeper truths. There is no *empowerment* without going through *show*. The ministry would be less fruitful, because of the unprepared vessel.

This is the first stage where the new believer would be called to address the public; be in the public eye and serve in public. This is the only stage where working and serving will be put into the heart by the Father. Until this stage, the Holy Spirit has not called us to be set apart[214] for service or cleared us for takeoff. Consider a surgeon. Many hours of college training and finally classroom learning nears completion. The surgeon is not yet ready to operate on people; there is a time of hands-on training to supplement the classroom training. We would not want a surgeon to operate until they have proven themselves able and until they have passed all of the education milestones set forth by the governing body. In that same manner, we will not serve the Father in power until we have grown through the prior stages and can *show* by silent example that the Holy Spirit is flowing not from us but through us. Only then can we *share* and only then can we be an affective worker in God's kingdom, because only then will it be obvious to others that God is in us.[215]

The Journey of Share

Every miracle of God—every act from God through us—is God *sharing* his love, personality, and nature. *Sharing* is not just *speaking*; it is ministry. It is honoring what he has birthed in us and allowing him to flow through us. Nothing else works. Nothing else produces his fruit. We will do well to stand firm with the position that nothing less than his flowing through us is acceptable when we *share*.

Miracles Associated with Share

In Acts 2:40–41,[216] Peter *shared* under the power of the Holy Spirit, and about three thousand were brought to salvation that day. In the Bible, the book of Acts has many examples of *share* and associated fruit.

The Journey That is Distant from Share

A *student* progressing through *hearing, believing, asking, receiving, doing, caring,* and *showing* but still remaining distant from *sharing* may be resisting or may not yet be called. They may be so humbled by what God is doing and is able to do that they feel unqualified. Many examples from the Bible can show that God does not call the qualified so much as he qualifies the called. God knows that we may feel unable to fulfill the call. This is a great perspective, because then we will be solely dependent upon him for all of the needs to fulfill the call. Read the biblical book of Jonah to see that Jonah did not feel qualified. He did not have the mind of God about the city of Nineveh and tried to run, but God knew he was prepared. God sent a whale to drive home the point that it was not Jonah doing the work, but God had a Word to *share* through him and he really wanted him to go. Moses felt unqualified, so God used Aaron and Moses as a team.[217] Gideon did not feel qualified and desired God to undeniably prove that he was *hearing* God's call,[218] so God confirmed his call twice using dew.

If we are not sure we are *hearing* God's call, we can be distant from *sharing*. We are stuck in *showing*. If we suffer from timidity, we may shy away from *sharing*. If the enemy has convinced us that there is too much pain in *sharing*, we may avoid progressing to that stage and live in pain management.

Blockages to Share

Emotional pain in the past cripples many a life from feeling that they would be useful in the slightest degree, regardless of how God wants to use them. This is pure deception, but certainly it can shackle the unaware *servant*. Pain in the past can be distorted by the deceiver of our lives and convince us that pain would be in the future; that failure would be in the future. He can lie to us with statements similar to, *"You have never been able to talk to your father about Jesus. He beat you and berated you the last time. He will do it again, so do not even try."* This kind of deception by the enemy builds a stronghold of timidity that must be broken down by truth and love. A sound mind is needed to press on, and God would desire that deliverance for his glory and our joy.

Leadership holding too tightly to an agenda, which does not match God's agenda, will squash maturity in the *student*. Leadership with God's heart will sense the maturation, affirm the call of the *student*, and either find a place for the call or allow God to develop something through their leadership.

For the larger vision, God's timing may hold back those who have seen the vision of a new call that is not yet come to its appointed time. God may be waiting on others to join in a larger vision or mobilization effort.

The Journey towards Share

God must cause this growth.[219] The *student* must get a *revelation* from God that they need to *share* and then *desire* to *share*. Prayer helps prepare hearts to *share*. The journey towards *embracing* this *step* is enhanced tremendously by others who have already made that journey. God will use them to encourage us and establish or remove boundaries for us to serve. *Seek* a mentoring arrangement from those who are more mature.

How Do We Start to Share?

The *student* must *invite* this *step* and be willing to *share*. Look for God to bring those before us who need to *hear* what God has taught us. God will do this for his glory and not for ours. When we are *sharing* what God has taught us, his power is flowing through us. We are not the power; we are the vessel. Like a light bulb, we are ineffective without the power. Yielding to the power we produce excellence; we produce light; and we produce truth.

Changing the Heart to Share

Allow God to remove barriers preventing you from *doing* what he has called you to *do*. By the time you reach this *step*, you have a relationship with God and you are able to participate in dialogues, not just monologues, with him. Ask him to show you barriers and then to help you remove them. His deep desire is to have all people be vessels for his glory. In doing so, we become filled with joy at being used.

The Challenge to Share

The *student* must not only *permit* but also *embrace* and be *changed* by the *sharing step*. Psalm 127:1[220] makes it clear that unless God *sends*, we go in vain. Ask God if you are ready to be *sent* out to *share*. Are you willing, or are you resisting? Your gifts will make room to be used. God will open the doors. Are you ready and willing? He has made you able. You can do all things through Christ who strengthens you.[221] What is God maturing in you? Are there places to serve in the local church? Are you *seeking* a place to serve? Are you open to serving? Are you willing to serve? Are you eager to serve?

In Matthew 22:37–40, Jesus told us that there were two statements that summarized all of the law and prophets: love God and love others as yourself.[222] These two commands give power to "The Great Commission."[223] This commission *sends* us into the entire world to *share* the news of God's love and his desire for us to return to him. God has *equipped* you with truth. He will call you because he has *equipped* you and qualified you. He chooses the weak in the world to confound the strong and wise.[224] Prove to him that he is right. Prove to yourself that he is right. *Share*.

If you have recently *accepted* Jesus Christ as Savior and Lord and have been diligently walking out his Word in your life, your heavenly Father desires that you *share* what he has done for you, in you, and through you.[225] Once you were blind, and now you can see.[226] God wants you to *share* what he has done. He wants you to testify. Do not embellish or stretch the truth; just *share* the facts. This is part of the process of overcoming the enemy.[227]

This is the *step,* which testifies to others about what God has done and is different from the *step* of *speaking* in the s*ervant process.* This effort is where others have the opportunity to identify with your situation, your test, and your testimony. This *step* is where your friends and family can listen with interest, because they most notice that *change.* They can authenticate the *transformation* and be inwardly challenged by the *change.* They may even be able to testify of your apparent hopeless situation or lifestyle, be undeniably shaken by the *change* in you, and shaken from their own unbelief.

Now is the time to open your mouth and to *share* the truth of your testimony. This is part of the process where you and your household can be saved.[228] In John 4:53, the royal official testified about what God had done, because of his faith and his entire household *believed*.[229] His family had to *believe,* because of his testimony of undeniable facts.

If you are a believer and God has been *teaching* you to walk out his Word and you are walking in holiness, he wants you to enter this time with eager anticipation and exhilaration! He is *teaching* you something new and is getting ready to *send* you out to *share.* You cannot give away what you do not possess. God has planted much in you, and you have allowed him to cause you to mature. Get ready to be used by him for a mission that will touch lives. He has taught you something to *share* and to give away. This will be powerful testimony, because it will be *empowered* testimony.

Some of the most *affective sharing* is what God taught most recently.[230] He will build upon the foundation he has taught you in the past, desiring that you *accept* what he *teaches* you now, so you can be a vessel to *share* a liberating, God glorifying truth into a situation at the last hour.[231] Your testimony will be about what he just taught you, and perhaps you will *share* with those you do not know. You will testify to those God puts in your path. You will find your most *affective* tool is what he just taught, whether that be how to *speak, caress, offer, bless, teach, mend, empower,* or *send.* The power in your ministry right now will be to use what he just taught you, and to use it in *share* mode as testimony.

Promotion beyond Share

Promotion from God will not come until the *student celebrates* the growth and *worships* God as the changer. At this time of promotion, the *student* is *sharing* what God has done in them and what he has recently taught them. During this *step,* the *student* will testify that God is the Lord of life. The *student* has the *revelation* to love the Lord God with all of their heart, mind, soul, and strength and to live for his glory.

God desires that the *student seek* him for the next *step* of growth, which is the *role* of the *servant.* The *student* has *celebrated sharing,* and now God wants them to get the *revelation* of the need to become a *servant.* He wants to develop the *student* into a *servant,* which is a very significant promotion from the *student step* of *shar-*

ing to the *servant step* of *speaking*. He will take action to promote that *revelation* in the *student* and will wait. Due to the maturity of the *student* and the need for *servants* in the field, it is possible that the rate and amount of growth may accelerate. Growth appearing unimaginable in the *student's* past may pale compared to the growth that God will put before them when they *accept* the new *role*.

Reflections and Discussion

Please reflect on the questions presented in the section titled "Main Discussion Guide for the Student Process" on page 194. Additionally, the following questions focus on *share*:

1. What might be going on in your life if you can *show* but not *share*?

2. How effective is it to *share* what God has just recently taught you?

3. What does it look like in your daily life to *share* what your heavenly Father has revealed to you?

4. When we start *sharing* what God has revealed to us with others, what does the enemy attempt to do? What does that look like in your interactions?

Expanding the Student Process

Prior to reading this section, it may be valuable to have a basic understanding of the *steps* and flow of the *student process*. This section expands each *student step* into more-detailed components, and presents diagrams to visualize the expansion. Every *step* in the *student process* has three *seasons*: *revelation, transformation,* and *celebration.*

Every *step* of *student* growth begins with a *season* of *revelation* from God, followed by a *season* of *transformation* with God as the main focus, and culminates with a *season* of *celebration* of the *change.* This is presented in outline form below.

I.	*Revelation Season*	Recognizing that God is the answer
	• Revelation	From God, of the need
	• Revelation	From God, of his provision to meet that need
	• Accept	God's provision as the only way to meet the need
	• Desire	God's provision to meet the need
	• Invite	God's provision to meet the need

Note: God will not move a *student* into the *transformation season,* unless the *student* invites. The invitation permits God to open the door and the *transformation season* can begin.

2. *Transformation Season*   Being Changed by God
   - Permit   God's way
   - Embrace   God's way
   - Change   As Gods wants

3. *Celebration Season*   Honoring the *transformation*
   - Celebrate   God's change
   - Worship   God as the changer
   - Seek   God for more of his growth

The victory of arriving at the *celebration season* may be quick for some *students* and slow for others. To a *student* who is good soil, the *revelation* season of the *hearing step* may be satisfied in moments; yet other *students* may grow at a slower rate. When contemplating their progress, the speed of tectonic plates may come to mind. *Servants* working one-on-one with hurting lives encounter *students* struggling to get through the *revelation season*. For example, a *student* may spend a long time in the *revelation season* just to move from the *desire* to *hear* to the *invitation* to *hear*. Their lives may have been decimated by the enemy, and the victory for those *students* may take years and seem difficult, meticulous, and laborious.

The target is not the *transformation season*; the target is the *celebration season*. *Celebration* is the indication of spiritual joy about the *change* that is planted in the heart. The victory is getting to the *celebration season*.

An example is presented using all three *seasons* of the *step, while* learning to *receive* the truth about eternal life through the blood sacrifice of Jesus Christ.

1. *Revelation Season*: The *student* must get a *revelation* of the need to *receive* what they just *asked* for. Then they must get a revelation that God can meet that need by *blessing* them with eternal life; then, they have to *accept* that God's provision is the only way. Following that, they have to *desire* that way ("God, I want to *receive*

Jesus Christ as Savior") and then *invite* the process, ("God, I actually cross that line and *receive* your truth, your way, and your life.")

2. *Transformation Season*: They must *permit* themselves to *receive*, to *embrace receiving,* and to be *changed* by *receiving.*

3. *Celebration Season*: They celebrate the *change,* worship God as changer, and then seek God for more growth. According to his schedule and purposes and for his glory, God will begin preparing the *student* for the next *step* in the *student process.*

Regardless of our maturity in the Lord, we always have something to learn, more lands to conquer.[232] Even though we may *operate* well in the *servant role*—when we find ourselves in one of the *student steps*—we are a *student,* and God is trying to *teach* us something for his glory and our joy. Even the greatest of us all go through the eight *student steps* in order to grow and give God more glory. Be aware of this consideration, as the rest of the book is presented. Even as a *servant* when the reference is to a *student,* it may be addressing the *servant* who is learning something new.

**The Expanded Student Step:
3 Seasons & 11 Periods**

Revelation from God

1. Revelation — of the need
2. Revelation — of God's provision
3. Accept — God's provision
4. Desire — God's provision
5. Invite — God's provision

Transformation from God

6. Permit — God's way
7. Embrace — God's way
8. Change — God's way

Celebration honoring change

9. Celebrate — God's change
10. Worship — God as the changer
11. Seek — God for more of his growth

The table above is abbreviated for simplicity and shown below.

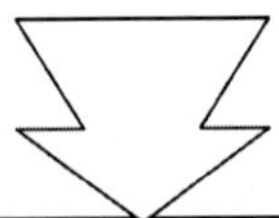

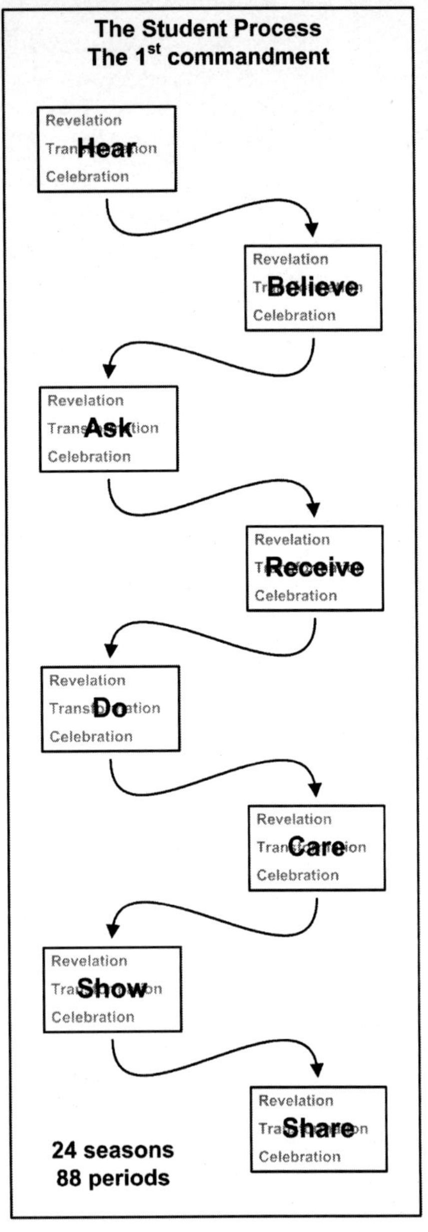

Revelation
Transformation
Celebration
Student Growth

The first growth step of HEAR is at top right.

All 8 steps of the Student Process are combined together to show a learning experience.

God uses this process to teach us the first commandment.

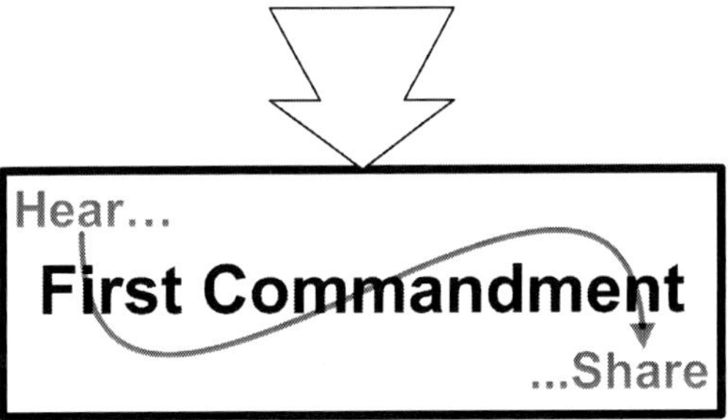

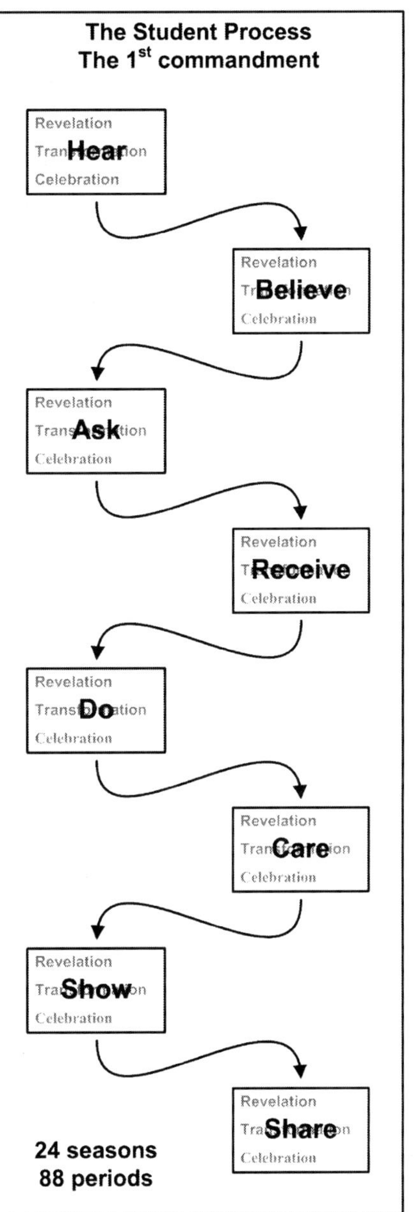

From Revelation to Victory for the Student

God gave the poem below directly to me by *revelation*. It presents a *student* at the beginnings of the *revelation season* and on through the *celebration season*. Notice the *student* who needs to offer everything to God, instead begins by offering a flake of paint. He is giving all he can, at first thinking the flake is all there is to give. Deeper *revelation* occurs, the entire life is given to God, and the victory is in progress. Read and be blessed, motivated, energized, and ignited.

The Season

A season is a day or two,
It is a life of change;
Of weeks or months in pits and ruts
And climbing out again.

It goes beyond appearances
And digs down to the soul
And fills the heart with healing
And makes one closer to whole.

It is a time of life and death;
A death of what must die
To make one more like Jesus Christ,
So He can lift you high.

The death is getting off the throne
And giving up the lie,
Which says the plans you made alone
Are not given to God to die.

New plans slowly come to light;
New ideas start to reign,
As God in His calm wisdom shows
That you've been born again.

Get the mop; the tears will flow,
As that which is death must die,
As kingdoms in the seasoning heart
Realize they were living a lie.

Repentance comes, and grief is full—
Joy and hope and fear
And calmness and assurance reign,
And angels start to cheer.

They cheer because the hope is there,
The hope of one cleansed life,
Which focuses now on the Throne of God
As the source and giver of Light.

"Somewhere beyond the pain and sadness;
Somewhere beyond the grief;
Somewhere beyond the depth of repentance
Is the path God set for me.

I know it is there, I trust in Him
And reject my worldly thoughts
That set me on this course of death
And had me doing 'Thou Shalt Nots'."

On it goes, as the heart just grows,
As God cultivates that seed
Of growth and change and purity,
And that heart just loudly pleads,

"God I need you now, to show me how;
I must reach out to you!
There is no other way to grow
And by myself I have no clue."

On it goes the refining of silver,
Seven times purified by Him.
Each time to a willing soul,
Yet it is painful giving up old sin.

Deep in the innermost parts of man,
Deep within a life of mistake,
It is paint on the throne of a sinful heart
That must be burned off flake by flake.

Each flake must be inspected
By the heart that will not let go,
And God patiently waits
For you to bring it to the throne

To put it in the refining furnace,
So it can be burned up,
And you can stand there weeping,
Or turn and receive the cup.

Of fellowship with the God of Love
And hope and joy and peace,
And talk to the One who purifies
And drop quickly to your knees.

As the flakes of the paint on this unholy throne,
Get burned up one-by-one,
Eventually it becomes clear to the heart
That the pain of letting go is gone.

Stride is quick to that throne of death
To grab the whole thing and offer it to God
And beg of Him to take that thing
That used to be your facade.

The New Walk begins
With a clarified view of life
And a request to the Lord above
To fill my life with Christ.

The Season is over,
Or did it just begin?
Did God just rebuild a life
To serve Him once again?

Did a proud heart just get off its throne,
Offer it to God with faith and reason,
Focus on humbly serving Him alone,
And put an end to the Season?

There is a time for everything,
A time for calling out,
A time for lifting up,
And a time for the faithful shout.

There is a time for marching round the walls
And a time for suffering.
There is a time for praying in faith
And a time for offering.

There is a time for growth in Love
With prayer, faith, and reason,
A time for repairing connections above,
A time known as "The Season."

Servant Role:
Giving God Away

This second half of the book describes the *role* of God and his *servant*, as noted in the "Speak To Share Method" diagram on page 179. The *servant role* is God moving through man to cause growth and maturity in *students* and therefore being an *affective servant* for him. The *affective servant* consistently wins the hearts of *students* and influences them to grow into *affective servants* themselves, repeating this method of growth.

God desires for us to always grow. He uses this *servant process* of eight *steps* to cause the *student* to grow and promote their growth to the next level. When God promotes a person to this *servant role*, he is growing and *equipping* the promoted to be a spokesperson for him.

The *student process* (already covered) teaches the *student* the first commandment, "*Love the Lord your God with all your heart, mind, soul, and strength.*"[233] By building the trust and love relationship with the Father, a relationship that never ceases to pull us higher. The *servant process* is a giving *role*; one that exemplifies the second commandment of "*Love your neighbor as yourself.*" As man, when we walk out this *role*, we are walking out the second commandment and giving the love of God away to cause *change* and growth in others.

God promotes from the *student role* into the *servant role* and then leads and guides his children through that *role*. The *servant* is challenged to review these eight *steps* and consider how far God has promoted them. Understanding their *step* of maturity will help them understand the people God puts in front of them for ministry. It will help them see where they are *empowered* by God and can serve most *affectively*.

Each *step* of the *servant process* is cumulative and durative. Each *step* when learned and repeated is a foundation for the next *step*. When a foundation piece crumbles, the *servant* is in danger of sliding backward in faith, faltering, or representing our Father in a less than excellent manner.

Progressing from Student to Servant

We prove ourselves diligent and fruitful to get promoted from the *student* to the *servant* and become a vessel for God. God wants the *servant* to be a vessel for his greatness to minister most effectively to the *student*. For God to reach the *student*, the *servant* will be taught to

Speak		The way he needs them to communicate;
	Caress	The gentle way he wants to touch lives and hearts;
Offer		The truth, rewards, and awards of God's *change* in God's way;
	Bless	The way that God wants to reveal himself;
Teach		Truth in God's way—the way that works best;
	Mend	The way that God wants emotional healing accomplished;
Empower		The way that God wants the Spirit to work; and then
	Send	The way that God wants commissioning to happen.

We are filled with joy, seeing growth, and we focus on removing obstacles to growth. Some of this *change* from *student* to *servant* and from *student* to God-vessel is evident when reading Romans 10, as explained after the "Speak To Share Method" on page 179. The heart of the *servant* overflows with prayers like, "God, let others see you, your hope, your vision, your mission, and your enthusiasm!"

Jesus told us to go into the world and preach.[234] Jesus tells us that we are sent to *share*, but when we *share*, we do well to recognize that we are commissioned by the Father to *speak* his truth. Those that (*hear* and) *believe* and are baptized will be saved.[235] The next effort for the *student* after being sent to *share* is the training to *speak* on behalf of God. Once trained, we begin functioning in the *servant role*. There is good news when we enter this phase of being the *servant*. This is where growth really begins. This is similar to children graduating from school and thinking that they have learned it all and are prepared for life, only to find out that they just have the credentials to begin doing some serious learning about how to put it all together and make use of their education in a public forum, hoping to be productive. The one who graduates from the *student role* to the *servant role* and from *sharing* to *speaking* might feel that they have learned it all, because they have learned so much; then they find out they have just reached the plateau of being able to serve the living God in humble power and are at the beginning of growth that will be the most exciting ride of their life.

The first time we are sent through the *student process*, we are to learn and also walk out the first commandment; to love him with everything we are. We learn that he can be trusted for eternal life and provision during the missions he gives us. The good news is that we will be sent through the *student process* multiple times. After salvation, we are sent through these *steps* to learn how to be like him and serve as he desires. This is part of his desire to get us to be clean vessels.

Some have tried to tell God how things really work. They waste much energy, trying to change the order of things and telling God how to do his job. God, who invented, creates, and develops all things needs no training. There are certainly times in our lives when we do try to teach him, but he just never has any "*Ah, Ha*" moments with us. He already knows all things and instead desires to *teach* us! As the *student* who is becoming the *servant*, we need awareness and training about this new *role* and how best to *operate* in these activities authored by God.

With great excitement, we dance up to the Father of life, ready to *share* what he has implanted in us, and we suddenly become aware that we need to be more *equipped*. This growth is where we mature from living out the first commandment into learning to live out the second commandment to love others as ourselves and *show* them our living Lord. As we mature through the last *student step* of *sharing* and progressing from *student* to *servant*, God will *teach* us the first *step* in the *servant role*: how to *speak* for him. His method for that is for us to become the *student* again, going through his eight *steps* to become gifted in *speak*. It is at this stage when the *student* must learn how to *speak* in God's anointed timing—using his anointed words—in his anointed way. He will *teach* us how to *speak* based on our giftedness. Becoming the *student* again means that we will find ourselves in the various stages of *hearing, believing, asking,* and so forth, all because the Father wants us to *speak* the way he wants us to *speak* and not necessarily in the way we were taught by the world to *speak*. When he has taught us to *speak*, we are mature and can *speak* for him. We are candidates, available *servants* for God, to be sent out to *speak,* because we have been commissioned to do so by the Father of truth.

Since all have fallen short of his glory,[236] we don't automatically know how to *caress* in ways that he desires. By God's *revelation*, we will realize that if we are to produce his fruit, we must *caress* his way and that we lack the awareness of how to accomplish that. His next *step* will be to *teach* us to be gentle and to *caress* the only way that works; his way, and realize that we find ourselves going through the *student process* again.

God will prune and strengthen us through each *step* of growth in the *servant process*. We will repeat the eight *step student* journey again to prepare us for the next role of servanthood. Each *step* of growth will see us being taught something wonderful, as God prepares us for humble service. This will continue as we mature through the rest of the *servant steps* of *offering, blessing, teaching, mending, empowering,* and *sending.* For God's glory, he puts us through the *student process* for each *step* of our growth in becoming his *servant.* This is the ultimate in being *transformed* by the renewing of our minds.[237] This growth is what he desires as he promotes maturity in us.

As we grow into the *teach role*, he can commission us and place us as teachers or pastors. A word of caution is presented here. When God plants an idea about doing something and has not *sent* the *servant,* it is a vision or dream, but not yet a mission or commission. An example is being excited about being a teacher. Unless God *sends* the *servant* out, being a teacher is still a dream.[238] If he has not yet *sent* the dreamer, they are still in *student* mode, learning to *hear, believe, ask, receive, do, care, show,* or *share;* or in *servant* mode learning to *speak, caress, offer,* or *bless.* The point to consider is that God has not *sent* the *servant,* so they are not yet commissioned to *share.* It is important to determine if the *servant* is going where they have not been *sent.* This will help resolve if they are *doing* what they have not yet been commissioned to *do.*

As we grow into the *mend role*, he may be commissioning us to be placed into *roles* like pastoral care, Stephen Ministry, or professional counseling—a ministry that gently steers lives by one-on-one interaction.

As we grow into the *empower role*, he may be commissioning us to be placed into a position of encouragement to the body, perhaps as an evangelist or administrator or other role of leadership. These *servants* energize and motivate a *student* to walk out their new life.

As we grow into the *send role*, he may be preparing us to be in church leadership, church administration, or other leadership roles. The list of what God can do with a willing, mature *servant* is just about endless, as we will see in the last days.

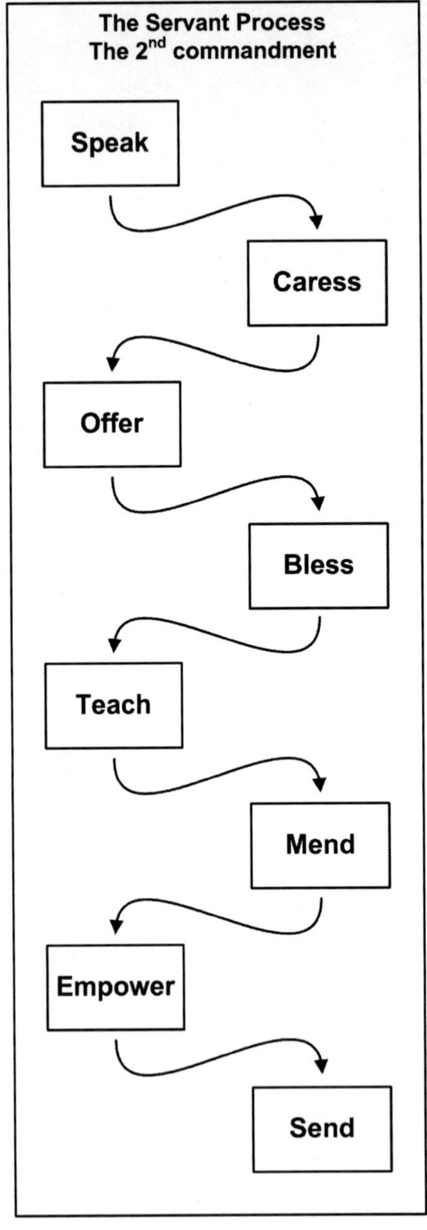

Diagram 5—The Servant Process
How God builds a servant, teaching them to serve.
Each step of growth prepares the servant to nurture students in a new way.
Copyright 2010 Michael Marburger

The Servant Process
The 2nd commandment
Speak
Caress
Offer
Bless
Teach
Mend
Empower
Send

The Resistant Student

God always desires to provide insight that is profound and deeper than man's initial understanding of his truth. Understanding the interactions between *servant* and *student* shines a light on some of that profound and deeper wisdom. At each of the eight *student steps*, there may be situations between them where the *student* is resisting growth. The awesome news is that God does not give up, if growth is not occurring or if the growing opportunity is rejected. The beauty of this growth is becoming aware that just like forgiveness, where Jesus tells us that we are to forgive seventy-seven times,[239] God desires to repeat and repeat and repeat and repeat, until the *student* grows.

Interaction with people occurs frequently in the *servant roles*, including teachers, counselors, prayer partners, hospital visitors, and pastors. In *sharing* and encouraging there is frequent feedback—both verbal and in body language—that communicates *student* growth or lack thereof. Recognizing progression of a *student* through the maturing process helps the *servant* know how best to serve. In the "Beneficiaries of the Role of" and "Resistance to the Benefits of" sections in the following chapters, consider how far the *student* has progressed through the process. For example, if they are not evidencing *belief*, are they perhaps still in the *hearing step*? What will God be doing if they do not *believe*? To help determine the maturity of the *student*, consider what God is doing. Is God in *caressing* or still in the *speaking role*? The *affective servant* observes and determines what God is doing to realize what *step* the *student* is working through and whether the *student* is progressing. The *affective servant* will do whatever God desires to cause growth in the *student*.

The Fallen Student

Broken hearts, broken hopes, and broken dreams can be used by the enemy to get *students* to doubt God's provision. This does not disappoint our Father. He sees that they have been dragged backward from *care* mode all the way to giving up on *believing* and wandering in an emotional catastrophe back in *hear* mode. The wounded *stu-*

dent now flails in lack of faith and trust in God's provision, which is the very truth that can set them free. This builds a callousness that resists *hear* and *believe*. They *hear* truth, yet resist *believing*, because they've been tricked by the enemy into believing that they've tried that path before; and it failed. They are in pain, because from their perspective, God did not come through for them this time. Their lack of *believing* is actually them taking control as part of pain management—to avoid pain in the future.

God does not want them in this state of turmoil and will *speak* and *caress* over and over and over again. God may even have to wait, until the wound is healed or gone before he presses the matter in his gentle way. He will strive to redeem the situation and return the *student* to an even more-firm trust and faith. The *student* must leave the past in the past and press onward toward the goal of knowing God is his fullness.[240]

Promotion from Student to Servant

Promotion by God from a *student* to a *servant* is less about the *servant* and more about other needy *students* and the fields ready for harvest.[241] Jesus, the *servant*, went after the one sheep,[242] one *student*. Jesus said to Peter, the *servant* he was training, "*Feed my sheep.*"[243] Promotion by God within the *servant process* is more about reaching additional *students*[244] [245] than about elevating *servants* in the public eye.

The Troubled Student Becoming
the Powerful Servant

God gave the poem below directly to me by *revelation*. It presents God *speaking* to a troubled *student*, calling them to let him *change* them, so they will become a powerful *servant*. The first part of the poem is a corrective word to wake the *student* to a problem. The last part of the poem, starting with "When you are *transformed*," is God revealing how far he wants to take the *servant* when they mature. This is shared here to example the significant difference between where we may be and where God desires us to arrive. Read and be blessed, motivated, energized, and ignited.

Mountains

Why is it some I've called to me
Lose their way and soon give up?
Why do they not persevere
And from me receive the cup?

Why do my plans for their prosperity
Come to close without my fruit,
And gifts that I have given to them
Get released as pillage and loot?

Why can I make it clear to you
Then watch you wander away,
After I had just promised you prosperity
And ask you to find shelter in me and stay?

How can you hear Truth from me
And let it go without performing its task?
Truth waits for you to be ready
To trust completely and believe and ask.

With all the truth I've spoken to you
And the way I have shown you my hand,
Why will you not be renewed in me,
So you can be a vessel to heal the land?

Take heed of my call, and listen to my chastisement,
It is meant to draw you to me. (Psalm 23:4)
My Word to you is to purify your life,
And restore you to what I created you to be.

I call to you and lift you up
And bless your steps in me,
So why do you partake in the light of Truth
And, though in my presence, do not see?

How many times should I call you,
Watch you mix untruth with my calling forth,
See you lose heart and wander aimlessly,
And from your lips, hear the unfaithful report?

I must turn your head to see this sin.
I must call you to task on this.
I must show you where you are failing,
So you can continue to be blessed!

My standard has not changed,
I've called you as my own,
And when you hear my truth, then doubt,
We are separate, and you…are alone.

I don't want to leave you,
But I'm nowhere near your sin.
My calling is for your victories
And to restore you once again.

I will not demand that you see this,
I will not force my hand.
I will offer truth for you to see,
And it's offered with no reprimand.

Here is my Word to you,
The Word that sets you free.
It will mend your heart and your life restart,
So you can be the BEST that you can be!

Don't listen to your past!
Don't listen to a chi!
Don't listen to the hurts in life.
They will distract your face from me.

I'll say it again, just study and think.
My desire is for you to see
That every Word I utter to you
Will draw your life to me.

Attend to what you hear,
And attend to what you think.
Grab hold of it, and inspect it carefully
To discern truth and from that, drink.

Throw out old thoughts that you concluded were truth
Many days ago,
Because the answer to, "How's that working for you?"
Sounds like, "I don't know." (mumbled)

Truth that comes from me
Does not steer you wrong.
It purifies the situation
And affirms that to me you belong.

Test the truth, and test the spirit,
They will always point to me.
If there is any part that does not fit love,
Just put it down, and from that word, flee.

Just as you turn your face to the warm sun,
Because it warms your skin,
Turn your face and heart to me
To daily let your life begin.

Seek out the truth that agrees with my Word,
That Word that washes clean.
Let it purify your past and present,
And I will show you my dream.

When you are transformed this way
The enemy will lose his hold
On the victories he used to have in your life,
Because of the lies he's told.

You will launch into the future
With a focus on only me,
And touch the eyes of the blind
And because of me they will see.

You'll seek out wisdom,
And get the gold of life,
And healing will be in your shadow,
And people will stop running to hide.

"Clear-headed and protected by God,"
Will be the label of choice
As the demon-filled, walking dead
Confront you with their loud voice.

Victory after win
Will be my gift to you,
As you sift the truth from facts,
And your life, I will renew.

The dead will rise; I have called it so,
Come to me to be empowered and used.
I will do this through you to fan my flame
And restore life to those once confused.

Never let go, and neither will I.
Know that I will change the clouds for you.
When you believe and speak by me,
Earth and wind and even water will move.

I am the rebuilder of that which was lost.
I restore and redeem and reclaim.
When you are clean to do my work,
You will see miracles in my holy name.

The waters will part, and earth will move,
Because my power to accomplish my Word is in you.
When I speak through your lips in these days of awe
Plants will grow, limbs of flesh will be restored,
    and hearts will be born anew.[246]

Forgiveness will run rampant,
Like a spiritual firestorm,
And bondage delivered by the killer of souls
Will be broken as the daily norm.

Humble Power will serve you
To affect the miracles I need
To steer my body through this coming time,
As I draw every one, who will come, to me.

When you rightly believe my Word,
I can do many things through you.
As you operate in my perfect truth,
You will speak, and the Mountains will move.

Reflections and Discussion

1. How can you tell when God is trying to *teach* you something?

2. Regarding the fallen *student*, what are some examples of broken hearts, broken hopes, and broken dreams that get people to doubt God's provision?

3. What do you think it means that these *steps* of growth are cumulative and durative? How does that apply to you?

4. What would you like God to do through you when you become an *affective servant*?

5. Why does God promote *students* to *servants*? Why would he be inclined to initially keep that more private than public?

Speak

Assertions about the Role of Speak

In the beginning (Read Genesis 1), God spoke. Everything begins with God *speaking*. His creativity is activated by his spoken word. What God *speaks* always accomplishes what he *sends* it forth to accomplish. His spoken word always accomplishes his desires.[247]

It is impossible for God to *speak* an untruth.[248] *Speaking* truth is an assertive, creative, active, and pursuing event. Christ being put to death on the cross is a *speaking* event pursuing the restoration of man. We are God's vessels on the earth. Our call will be to *speak* truth,[249] the Word of God, the words of Jesus Christ, and the word of truth about Jesus Christ.

Reasons for the Role of Speak

God *speaks* to *students* before they can *hear*. The *servant* of God *speaks* to *students* on God's behalf. This *speaking step* is where God *teaches* us to *speak* everything and only what he desires us to say to the listener. His Word, in his time and in his way for his reason and his glory, *changes* lives. Consider radio waves, which carry a particular radio channel. With our eyes, we cannot see the wave or the channel it carries, but it is there, and if the listener is prepared by having the right equipment, *hearing* can happen. Truth of heaven is sent to the *hearer*, embedded in the human voice, written Word, or other communication technique. We cannot see truth; we can just see the words and methods that represent truth. Flesh and blood cannot reveal truth; only our Father in heaven can.[250] God speaks our language, but it is not his native tongue. His native tongue is truth—the truth that created the universe, lifts hearts, heals, forgives, and *transforms*. His still, small voice—the radio channel being carried on the radio wave in the prior example—whispers gently, presenting truth. If the listener has been prepared, *hearing* can happen. The example of perfect *speaking* is Jesus Christ, who told us that he never spoke unless God had something to say through him.[251] Jesus did not utter idle words, and when we are in service to our Father, he desires to *teach* us to utter no idle words.[252] He desires us to *speak* just exactly what he wants to say so that his word can accomplish exactly that which he sent it forth to accomplish. When God uses the *servant* to *speak* his truth in his time in his way for his purpose and his glory, it is sent at a frequency the listener can *hear*. Only God knows what it takes for the listener to *hear* because only God knows the equipment of the listener and what the enemy may have done to damage the ability to listen.

A good example of God in the *speaking role* is Jesus' sharing the truth of heaven in parables, displaying examples of heaven in a way that prepared hearts are able to *hear* and perceive. Read Matthew 15:29–39 to see where Jesus fed the four thousand. This is an example of God *speaking* through miracles. Miracles fall into this *speaking step,* because these miracles are meant to prepare the listener to *hear*. A study of Matthew 5–9 reveals God's *speaking* and man's *hearing*. Miracles add legitimacy to the truth, reinforcing the word soon to be spoken or recently spoken. Isaiah 35:4[253] tells us to *speak* to those with fearful hearts, and as they *hear*, the miracles of God occur. The miracles of God legitimize the truth of God.

The *speaking step* is God communicating either to *affect change* or to *celebrate* truth. Worship accomplishes *speaking. Speaking* occurs so that the listener can *hear* the Word. It is pronouncement of truth, including miracles, upon unbelieving and believing ears. Preaching is the *speaking role*. Read the Bible to see that in Matthew 5–8, there are *speaking* examples, and only preaching and miracles are noted, because this is God in the *speak role*. Toward the end of Matthew

8, faith and belief are the results. *Speaking* is the *servant step,* which God uses to cause and allow the listener to *hear.*

Challenge to Accept the Role of Speak

God *equips* the *servant,*[254] and still they must *get* and *accept* the *revelation* that they have been *equipped* by God for the *role* of the *speaker.* The *servant* must *desire* and *invite* that *role* into their lives. While walking out the *role,* the *servant* must *permit* and *embrace* God *operating* through them and be used to effect *change* in *students.*

The Word says, *"Resist Satan and he will flee from you."*[255] Satan is a liar and the father of lies.[256] He is the foundation of deception. He is deception itself. How can they resist deception, unless they know the truth? How can they know the truth, unless someone *speaks* it? How can someone *speak,* unless they are *sent?*[257] Psalm 127:1[258] shares truth that unless God builds a house, they that labor build in vain. Unless God calls a thing to happen, those who make it happen waste their time. Do not *speak* on your own or go on your own; it will be fruitless. Wait for God to enable you and to *send* you.

As God causes growth, the truth will bubble inside and there will be a *desire* to let it out for his glory. The *servant* will want to learn how God wants them to *speak.* Will you go before your heavenly Father and ask him to *teach* you how to *speak* like he wants you to *speak: to speak* everything and only what he wants said in the manner and time that he desires it spoken? Has he caused you to have the fierce *desire* to *speak* his Word in his time in his way for his purpose and his glory? You are *invited* to *ask* him to give you a vision of the fruit that occurs when you *share* "no idle words;" then *ask* him to call you into that vision. *Speak* for God and say only what he wants you to say and everything that he wants to say through you, because his Word accomplishes his desire. *Accept* the challenge to *speak.*

Beneficiaries of the Role of Speak

God does not *speak,* unless he wants someone to *hear.*[259] When God *speaks,* he desires for the *student* to *hear.* The desired response to God's *speaking* is for the *student* to *hear* what he is saying. If God is in the *speaking* mode, he is seeking some *student* to *hear*. There is no other option, because God does not waste his time or merely entertain people that need his growth. He is always drawing his people to him, since they've been bought back for a price.[260] *Affective speaking* takes place only in God's timing and to those listeners prepared to *hear*, lest the *servant* be planting seeds in unfertile soil, on rocky ground, or on hardened paths.[261] Until the *student hears, speaking* is the only effort that really matters. *Caressing* and *offering* might be *accepted*, but they are not the primary effort. *Blessing, teaching*, or *sending*, for example, would be like casting pearls before swine,[262] because the recipient is just not prepared for them yet.

Resistance to the Benefits of Speak

When God moves the *servant* to *speak* and the *student* does not *hear*, the *speaking* of truth is repeated over and over in gentle wisdom. Consider a discussion between a *servant* and a *student*. In spiritual confusion the *student* says, "*I just cannot hear that right now,*" or "*Hey, just don't talk to me about Jesus Christ anymore.*" The *student* is stuck and will progress no farther in faith until *hearing* takes place. Until then, truth bounces off of the broken spirit and little else is *affective*. God's actions and the actions of his *servant* will remain in the *speaking step*. An example of God holding off *speaking*, until a time when the listener can *hear* is in 2 Samuel 11:27-12:1,[263] where God did not address David about his sin with Bathsheba, until after their son was born from the sin-laden relationship. *Affective speaking* is in God's time. God's truth in God's time hit David at the frequency of his spiritual ears, and in verse 13, David recognizes and speaks truth from God when he says, "*I have sinned against the Lord.*"

As a *servant*, observe for evidence that the *student* has never been in *hearing* mode, perhaps because truth has never been exposed to their ears. This is a case where the *student* just does not know the truth, because the truth has been kept from them. The *servant role* will be to *speak* truth over and over again—God's message in God's time with God's methods for God's reasons and God's glory.

As a *servant*, observe the *student* for evidence of resistance to *hearing.* Is the *student* in *hearing* mode or not? Is there some area in the life of a *student* where God seems to be repeatedly *speaking?* For example, a *student* might be involved in some rebellious sin, such as knowingly spending time with the wrong person, involved with sexual misconduct, or walking out of a marriage, which God wants to redeem. These are the times when God *speaks,* but the enemy has convinced them to close their ears and to not *hear*…yet! It is the *speaking* and *caressing,* which draw man to the lap of God. Satan was in the presence of God and heard truth. Satan knows truth and is not changed by it.[264] Not all souls are yet ready to *hear* truth and be *transformed.*

Promotion beyond Speak

Promotion from God will not come until the *servant* gives *glory* to God for being used in the *role, celebrates* the growth in the *student,* and *worships* God as the changer. At this time of promotion, the *servant* has learned to *speak* the words that God has taught them. During this *step,* the *servant* has learned that God has words of truth that must be communicated exactly on his schedule and his way for his reasons and his glory, and his spoken word always accomplishes his desires.

God desires that the *servant seek* him for the next *step* of *servant* growth, which is *caressing.* The *servant* has *celebrated speaking,* and now God wants them to get the *revelation* of the need to *caress.* He will take action to promote that *revelation* in the *servant* and will wait.

Reflections and Discussion

Please reflect on the questions presented in the section titled "Main Discussion Guide for the Servant Process" on page 195. Additionally, the following questions focus on *speak*:

1. What happens when we *speak* without God wanting us to *speak*? Compare that with what happens when we *speak* by his request?

2. How does your *role* change when someone rejects your *speaking*? How does your resolve change? How can you be sure you were sent to *speak* for them to *hear*?

3. What does it mean to filter all of your *speaking* through Psalm 127:1? How does Psalm 127:1 *affect* your method of *speaking*, as you are promoted to this *role* of *speaking*?

4. What does it mean to you that God's Word does not return to him void but accomplishes his purposes? As one in the *speaking role* for God, how does that *affect* your daily activities?

5. What does it mean to you to utter no idle words? How can that *affect* your daily life?

Caress

Assertions about the Role of Caress

Caressing is the *step* that turns rocks into soil. This *step* breaks down the fruitless heart to *transform* it into fruitful soil. This is God's gentleness[265] exhibited for us to begin to *believe*. He touches our lives with the most tender, loving, and gentle form of intimate touch, a *caress.*[266] This *caress* term embodies the fruit of the Holy Spirit.[267] When he touches our lives in his attempts to *caress* and reach us, he displays perfect consistency with the fruit of the Holy Spirit.[268] He will always display them, because he is the same yesterday, today, and forever.[269] He does not get violent or deviate from his character of love while pursuing us.[270] He waits to show us mercy.[271] God desires to reach and draw[272] every person to him. He tells us to go into the world and preach the gospel.[273]

Everything that God does is for his glory. For those with soft hearts towards him, he does not knock people on the side of their head or scare them into believing.[274] God desires to woo us with awareness of his benefits for life here on the earth[275] and of the benefits of continuing a relationship with him for eternity. His desire is to draw us to him[276] and not to whip us into shape, "slap us up side of the head," or demand that we come to him against our will. The enemy may provide a negative situation that our Father will use as an opening to reach us, yet our Father desires to reach us without the enemy corrupting our lives. Read Hebrews 12 to see that God will chastise the heart which is turned against him, but the desired result is a soft heart coming to him, because the path of the hard heart leads to destruction. He woos, calls, comforts, and encourages. He desires to reach every person, and his desire is to draw us to him. He calls us into his promises of prosperity not calamity.[277] *Caressing* is buried in the *sharing* of many teachers during a sermon, as they broadcast the gentle, safe truth meant to shower the *student* with a mist of peace and safety.

Reasons for the Role of Caress

The gentleness of God draws man to repentance. Man compares and realizes a discrepancy between what he's *heard* and what he is doing. That discrepancy shows him his sin, and the gentleness of God allows him to feel safe to repent and *seek* forgiveness. This cannot happen without the *caress* of God. Corrective action from God is meant to cause men to see the fruit of their path. When man realizes that the road he is on is faulty, he recalls the gentleness of God and *seeks* forgiveness and favor. In The Parable of the Prodigal Son (Read Luke 15:11–32), man is not meant to choose repentance as the lesser of two terrible choices: one being a life without God and the other being a life with a bitter, punishing God. Instead repentance comes when man realizes that it is right to throw down all bondages of sin and is safe to run to the Father for forgiveness and favor.

In Matthew 17:5[278] God *speaks* to the disciples saying, *"This is my Son, whom I love; with him I am well pleased. Listen to him!"* Note the tenderness in that statement. There are four parts of that sentence, and three of them are full of love and tenderness: "My Son," "love," and "pleased." The fourth matches that tone: "Listen to him" is a *caress*.

In Galatians 6:1, it is written, *"Brothers, if someone is caught in a sin, you who are spiritual should restore him gently."* We are shown an example of the Spirit of God flowing through a believer during a call for someone else to see sin and repent. The passage indicates that gentleness will be evident.

The Spirit of God always moves in a *caressing* mode to touch, reach, teach, and grow lives. Read Matthew 23 to see that when

Jesus encounters a hard heart fixed in religious ways that are not his own; in these cases, a different corrective voice is used. If God breaks a person, it is because of a religious heart that leads others astray. For the soft-hearted, he will not break a bruised reed.[279] Those with broken lives due to the enemy are bruised reeds that God will call back to his lap for healing and restoration. His desire is to woo us to come to him not whip us to come to him.

Challenge to Accept the Role of Caress

God *equips* the *servant*,[280] and still they must *get* and *accept* the *revelation* that they have been *equipped* by God for the *role* of the *caresser*. The *servant* must *desire* and *invite* that *role* into their lives. While walking out the *role*, the *servant* must *permit* and *embrace* God *operating* through them and be used to *affect change* in *students*.

Has God caused you to grow through the *role* of the *speaker*? Do you feel that inner urge and calling to exhibit the goodness and mercy of God and to *offer* his vast multitude of benefits? Do you feel the call to be as gentle as our living Lord to see each hurting and wounded person with the eyes of God filled with *desire* to *caress* and woo them to the heart of the Master? Ask God for the vision to see yourself being as gentle as he desires to *caress* and then *ask* him to call you into that vision.

Beneficiaries of the Role of Caress

The response to the *caress* of God is for the *student* to *believe* what God is saying. After truth is *heard*, God begins to *caress*. In that gentleness of the *caress*, the wounded soul finds safety and makes the choice to *believe*. It is in that safe time when the doubting venture out of their cocoon of confusion and trust in his unfailing love.[281] As *affective servants*, counselors see this in their office. As a *servant*, if you observe situations where God is exhibiting a *caress* towards someone, you will probably find someone needing to *believe* a new truth that God has revealed to them, which they may be struggling with. He is presenting the fruit of the Spirit[282] to allow them to see safety in his presence and to allow them to *believe* something he has spoken to them about.

The Forceful Who Miss Out on Caress

There are religions and churches that have their religious police. They seem to feel that their mission from God is to humiliate and force people into submission and to go into battle with them, until they comply with religious rules and behavior. Instead of people being *transformed* by the renewing of the mind,[283] the religious police seem convinced that people are *transformed* by the beating of the flesh, that confrontation and the resulting emotional pain will force others to *believe* in the goodness of God. Christianity has groups of people who act this way in error. This is living under the bondage of the law and religion as noted by Jesus in Matthew 23. Battle overpowers external actions, but love overpowers the internal heart; and *changed* actions are seen as the result. We cannot use the law as our target; we must use our Father in heaven as our target and have the result of our relationship with him be our behavior that matches or exceeds the law.[284] Beating our flesh into submission is related to us overpowering our own *desires* by the power of God doing the work in us.[285] Once again, this is a result not a target. Beating our flesh into submission is not being beaten up by someone else, physically or verbally, to force us to adapt to God's way of thinking.

Resistance to the Benefits of Caress

Consider the response, "*I just don't believe that,*" "*I don't believe it like you; that is for other people,*" or "*My religion does not believe that Jesus was God, so please stop trying to make me believe.*" Have not most eager bearers of truth encountered those kinds of comments? We cannot—and God will not—whip those people into *believing*. Gentleness is the answer. It is the goodness of God that draws men to *change*.

If *believe* does not happen in the *student, speaking* and *caressing* are repeated by the *servant*. The gentleness of God does not give up. Like a breeze, the spirit of gentleness safely surrounds the one in *hearing* mode, exhibiting that it is safe to *believe*. Over and over, the wind carries truth to the *student*. Since it is the gentleness of

God that draws man to repentance, the gentleness persists always in hope of the *student* entering into *believing*.

Promotion beyond Caress

Promotion from God will not come until the *servant* gives *glory* to God for being used in the *role*, *celebrates* the growth in the *student*, and *worships* God as the changer. At this time of promotion, the *servant* has learned to *caress* by *speaking* the words that God has taught them in the gentle manner in which the nature of God desires them to be communicated. During this *step*, the *servant* has learned that God has words, attitudes, and methods that work and man has those that fail.

God desires that the *servant seek* him for the next *step* of *servant* growth, which is *offering*. The *servant* has *celebrated caressing*, and now God wants them to get the *revelation* of the need to *offer*. He will take action to promote that *revelation* in the *servant* and will wait.

Reflections and Discussion

Please reflect on the questions presented in the section titled "Main Discussion Guide for the Servant Process" on page 195. Additionally, the following questions focus on *caress*:

1. How can God's role of *caressing* be important to hurting lives?

2. What *changed* in your thinking when you came to understand that the *caress* of God was a role he meant for you—that you were meant to communicate in soft and gentle ways?

3. Have you ever been confronted by religious people who were trying to compel you to *believe* something? What did you think of their *caress*? Have you ever been guilty of doing the same thing?

4. In what situation would *operating* in the role of the *caresser* produce verbal aggression from you towards someone?

5. How does *caressing* manifest, as we communicate his truth? What value is there in being gentle?

6. What are some of the ways that God might want to *change* the way you *caress* on his behalf?

Offer

Assertions about the Role of Offer

God *offers* to get the *student* into the *step* of *asking.*[286] God *offers* only the best,[287] including: hope,[288] eternal life,[289] abundant life,[290] the Holy Spirit,[291] spiritual power,[292] spiritual fruit,[293] the opportunity to allow him to be Lord in and through our lives, and a relationship with him. The truth in the scriptures is awesome, perhaps even startling, in that God does not put a limit[294] on what he *offers*, and appears to *offer* all[295] that he has, even his son Jesus Christ.[296] The abundant joy in this *role* is that there is no limit to what God will *offer* through the *servant*. Feel free to search the truth to find some limit on what God *offers* to his children who have their face humbly turned to him.[297] Notice the lack of limitations in edited portions of Ephesians 3:16–19,[298] *"Strengthen you with power… Christ may dwell in your hearts…that you…may have power…to grasp how wide and long and high and deep is the love of Christ, and to know this love that surpasses knowledge—that you may be filled to the measure of all the fullness of God."*

God *offers* everything we are moved by him to *ask* for.[299] When we realize our privileges as sons and daughters, it is no surprise that he would *offer* so much. The *offer* from God is to restore us to the kingdom joy,[300] position, and a relationship[301] that we were meant to be in from the very beginning. Read the Parable of the Prodigal

Son in Luke 15:11–32 for an example and note in verse 31, where the father says, "*All that I have is yours.*" The Prodigal son parable paints a powerful picture of this awesome heavenly truth.

Reasons for the Role of Offer

God is considerate of our free choice and does not force us to *accept* anything of his. His *offer* is always something good from heaven. All good and perfect gifts come from God.[302] All good and perfect gifts are *offered*, not mandated, forced, or shoved down our throat. This is the very beauty of love: to *offer* and not demand and to *seek* our *acceptance* and approval before transferring anything to us.

Demands and terrorism do not come from God. As documented in the Old Testament, Israel sinned and went astray from God many times. God invoked corrective actions to wake his people up, so they would come to him to *accept* what he never stopped *offering*. Read Isaiah 30:1–18 to see an excellent example of God *speaking* a corrective voice over his people, and he still ends at Isaiah 30:18 with, "*Yet the Lord longs to be gracious to you.*" Even while being rejected, his *offer* stands. That is a wonderful example of God's *offer*. By God's power, the *servant* in the *role* of the *offerer* will *offer* many times, because the Lord desires to be gracious to his people.[303] The *offer* from God is not to be retracted, except by God himself.[304]

It is vital to the *servant* to see that God will *offer* to the hurting soul, but he does not make demands to that hurting soul. Two verses in the NIV Bible document demands from God. One is Genesis 9:5,[305] where God tells us that he will demand an accounting from any man or animal that kills a man. The second is Psalm 25:10,[306] where God tells us that all the ways of the Lord are loving and faithful for those who keep the demands of his covenant. The latter verse reveals that keeping the covenant is a demanding, tough process but does not reveal a demanding Lord. An example is that the view from a mountain top is wonderful, but the climb is demanding. Only with the power of the Lord is it possible to climb his mountain, to keep the demands of his covenant. The reward of getting there is awesome. The *role* of the *offerer* is part of *equipping* the *student* for the climb.

Challenge to Accept the Role of Offer

God *equips* the *servant*,[307] and still they must *get* and *accept* the *revelation* that they have been *equipped* by God for the *role* of the *offerer*. The *servant* must *desire* and *invite* that *role* into their lives. While walking out the *role*, the *servant* must *permit* and *embrace* God *operating* through them and be used to *affect change* in *students*.

The enemy tries to prevent us from maturing into the *offer role* because he does not want us to participate in the effort to help the *student* to *ask*. *Seek* God to determine if he has matured you through *speak* and *caress*. Do you feel his passion to *offer* his unlimited love, grace, mercy, and favor to hurting wounded souls? Has he taught you to *offer* his good gifts? Teachers, counselors, evangelists, Bible study leaders, and preachers all *offer* the gift of truth wrapped by God in a manner specifically designed for his audience. Do you *hear* the upward calling to be in the *role* of the *offerer*? Are you *empowered* to walk out this role of *offerer*? That which you *offer* will be of great value to God. What God *offers* through the *servant* goes out with the gentleness of a *caress*. Will your *offer* match the gentleness exhibited by Jesus Christ, the author and perfecter of our faith?[308]

The best examples of what to *offer* are eternal life through Jesus Christ,[309] and the power of Holy Spirit[310] to *transform student* lives. God also *offers* gifts to complement and complete the whole body of Christ. God *offers* many benefits described in the scriptures that the enemy would hide from us. Are you being called by God to mature into this *role of offerer*? As a *servant* of God in the *role* of the *offerer*, God will exhibit no limitations with you as a vessel. The *offer* from God through you will be limited to and unlimited to the majesty of God and all he has. Enlarge your vision.[311] God has more to *offer* through his *servant* than his *servant* can perceive.[312]

Beneficiaries of The Role of Offer

The *student* has progressed from *hearing* to *believing* but has not yet entered into *asking*. Since truth is *believed*, the Father will *offer*. God wants the *student* to *ask* for the *offer*. God continues to *offer* by *speaking* truth in love until the *student asks*. The only fruitful response to the *offer* of God is to *ask* for what is being *offered*. This *step* requires motivation and an act of free will. Value must be seen by the *student,* or nothing will happen. They will not progress; they will not get to the next level.

Resistance to the Benefits of Offer

An *offer* from God is blocked by doubt and lack of firm belief. As a *servant,* are you able to discern that God is in *offering* mode towards a *student* over and over again? Observe to see if the *student* is in *asking* mode or not.

Consider the response, "*I cannot ask God for forgiveness. I've just done too many things wrong in my life. I've heard what you've said, and I believe what you said, but I just cannot ask him for eternal life. Thank you for telling me, but I'm I not ready to ask for eternal life.*" The response from God is to continue to *speak, caress,* and *offer* in his timing and not to progress to the next *step.* Progressing to the next *step* will not produce God's fruit, until the *student asks.*

Offers must come from God, never from our own *desires.* If our *desire* matches God's desire, we still must wait for God's timing for the *offer* to be sent to the one who is being prepared. We must wait until they are fertile soil. The *offer* is to the *student* who has already *heard* and *believed* but who the enemy may have damaged and inflicted with timidity about *asking. Offering* repeatedly in the flesh can remind the *student* that they are in rebellion and that may cause them to feel pressure from the enemy, to get to the next level. God applies pressure in ways that work long-term; the enemy does not. At this stage, the *student* will see God move in his perfect time to *speak* and *caress,* as well as *offer* over and over again. The message from God will be, "*See that I love you, and see what good I have promised for you! I invite you to reach out to me! This is a free gift I have for you.*"[313]

When the *student asks,* the Father will respond with *blessing.* When the *asking* is evident, such as, "*Jesus, I ask you to come into my heart,*" or, "*Father, I ask you to forgive me in Jesus' name,*" the response of what was in the *offer* is a *blessing* from God. God will move from *offering* to *blessing,* because he desires the *student* to enter, to the *step* of *receive, and* to get what was just *asked* for.

Promotion beyond Offer

Promotion from God will not come until the *servant* gives *glory* to God for being used in the *role, celebrates* the growth in the *student,* and *worships* God as the changer. At this time of promotion, the *servant* has learned to *offer* by letting God *operate* through them and *offer* the provisions and gifts of God that meet needs and give him glory.

God desires that the *servant seek* him for the next *step* of *servant* growth, which is *bless.* The *servant* has *celebrated offering,* and now God wants them to get the *revelation* of the need to *bless.* He will take action to promote that *revelation* in the *servant* and will wait for it to occur.

Reflections and Discussion

Please reflect on the questions presented in the section titled "Main Discussion Guide for the Servant Process" on page 195. Additionally, the following questions focus on *offer*:

1. Where are the scriptures that put a limit on what God wants to *offer* his children?

2. What limits does God place on what he is *offering* to his children?

3. Where will the *servant* role use demands to convince someone to *ask* for what God is *offering*? How easy is that going to be to implement in your life in every interaction, regardless of your frustration level?

4. What are some examples of the difference between an *offer* and a demand? Consider what happened the last time you put forth a demand, and whether people saw your heavenly Father during that time.

Bless

Assertions about the Role of Bless

Everything from God is a *blessing*. *Blessings* are intended to be *received*. *Blessings* are intended to affirm,[314] reinforce, strengthen,[315] support,[316] encourage,[317] and call believers upward to a higher calling[318] to allow them to exhibit the goodness of God.[319] *Blessings* can remind us of future promises,[320] reward us,[321] and feed a thirsty soul. Consider the *blessing* of God in Numbers 6:24–26: "*The Lord bless you and keep you; the Lord make his face shine upon you and be gracious to you; the Lord turn his face toward you and give you peace.*" Notice that all of these *blessings* are from God to his people. They are God giving out of his abundance and majesty. What is *blessing* in action other than abundance and majesty poured out from our heavenly Father toward us and upon us to reflect his glory and his desire for the good and encouragement of his children?

Grace is God giving us what we do *not* deserve. Mercy is God *not* giving us what we *do* deserve. Both are *blessings*, and all good and perfect gifts come from God.[322] We may not understand his perfection immediately, but someday we will. Answers to prayers are *blessings* from God. All answers from God are perfect, even if they do not match our desires. God redeems all things, and his answers may be beyond our understanding. God always answers prayers perfectly. Everything from God is a *blessing*.

Prayers are *asking* him for something or praising for his answers. When we *ask* God for something in prayer, God will answer and his answers are always good and perfect *blessings*. Read Matthew 5:3–11 for a study of the beatitudes to reveal that all of the *blessings* are pronounced toward believers. These *blessings* are broadcasted as truth, ready for prepared listeners to perceive.

Reasons for the Role of Bless

The *bless role* is how God gives without a measuring stick. God desires to *bless* us often by providing what he promised in the *offer*. He desires to pour and pour and pour into us. His desire is to restore us to what he originally designed for us before the fall in Genesis. He gives us everything that we are ready to *receive* or will *receive* from him, whether we are aware of his actions or not. Everything that ever comes from God is a *blessing* to get our attention and prepare us for the *teach* words to follow. The promises of God and the gifts of God are his way of *blessing* us for a purpose: to show us and others his plan, his kingdom, and his glory.

Challenge to Accept the Role of Bless

God *equips* the *servant*,[323] and still they must *get* and *accept* the *revelation* that they have been *equipped* by God for the *role* of *bless*. The *servant* must *desire* and *invite* that *role* into their lives. While walking out the *role*, the *servant* must *permit* and *embrace* God *operating* through them, and be used to effect *change* in *students*.

Has God caused your growth through *speaking, caressing,* and *offering*? Do you feel God's passion and calling to *operate* in this *role* and *bless students* that he puts in front of you, so they can *receive*? What does it look like for you to be a vessel of *blessing* into the life of an appointed *student*? The *servant* called to *bless* will be on fire with the abundance of God. People will flock around this *servant* and have a long list of reasons why, and some reasons might even be specific. There is just something about this *servant*, which draws people. This *servant* is an outlet for the Father, a funnel for his *blessing*, and a clean conduit for his service. Are you being called to be in the *role* of the *blesser*? God *blesses* by providing what he *offered*—the promises of God, and he will use his *servant* in the *bless role* to accomplish this. Pastors and teachers expressing the above and beyond favor of God are conduits of *blessing*.

Beneficiaries of the Role of Bless

The *blessing* is to be *received*. As a *servant*, observe the life of a *student* looking for God pouring out a *blessing*. Is the *student* in *receiving* mode? God always wants that *blessing* to be *received*. Are you seeing God's *blessing* over and over toward a *student*? God can *bless* in waves and waves for encouragement. He can also *bless* over and over to get attention. Observe to see that the *student* is in *receiving* mode for the outpouring of *blessings*. An example of *blessing* from God might be a supernatural healing of some disease, an outpouring of abundance to address an area of repentance, a special overflowing of abundance in a personal or professional life, or the power to *change* a life by *transformed* thinking. The *blessing* is to be *received* with gratitude and thanksgiving. After the *blessing* is *received*, God will follow with his *teaching*.

Resistance to the Benefits of Bless

What about the *student* who has grown through *hearing*, *believing*, and *asking* but who resists entering the *receiving* mode? *Blessings* not *received* are as effective as *blessings* not *offered*. Consider the conversation that ends in, "*I just cannot receive that.*" A favorite of the enemy, who lies to us and says we are not worthy, convinces us that we have to pay for our own sin by some self-abasement or to remove ourselves from God's presence. His lies produce a response that sounds like, "*I know God loves me, but with all of the people I have hurt (or killed), I am not ready (have not been punished enough) to receive forgiveness. I just have not earned (or performed enough or worked hard enough to deserve) it yet. I have encountered so many failures that God's favor must not be for me. I've asked for God's forgiveness, but I'm not ready to receive it yet.*" The truth of "*For freedom Christ has set you free*"[324] has not resonated within their spirit yet. God will continue to *speak, caress, offer,* and *bless* over and over and over and over, until the wounded soul sees truth and responds by *receiving* the *blessing* that God desires to pour out upon them. All good and perfect gifts come from the Father who loves us. Every answer from God is a *blessing*. Some answers to prayer are *blessings* (addressing sin), and it looks like chastisement to draw us to him. Psalm 23 tells us that his rod and his staff comfort us; they do not cast us away. Correction from God is a *blessing* from him to draw us to him.[325] God desires to turn things sent by the enemy into things for his glory, and this is accomplished by even more outpourings of *blessing* from heaven.

Another example is one who *asks* forgiveness for some act in which they were used by the enemy. The enemy still has them confused and after the *asking*, they continue to live in depression and brokenness because, though *asked* for, the forgiveness was not received. In this *step*, counselors have an opportunity to resolve an issue related to "*My people perish for lack of knowledge*"[326] by *speaking*, *caressing*, *offering*, and *blessing* and by presenting the fullness of what forgiveness is and does.

The wounded soul who *asks* and then does not *receive* goes no farther, until God's *blessing* is *received*. *Blessings* not *received* are as *affective* as *blessings* not *offered*. *Blessings* must be *received* to be effective. When the *student receives*, God can move from *blessing* mode to *teaching* mode, because he desires to move them to the next level of *doing*.

Promotion beyond Bless

Promotion from God will not come until the *servant* gives *glory* to God for being used in the *role*, *celebrates* the growth in the *student*, and *worships* God as the changer. At this time of promotion, the *servant* has learned to *bless* by letting God *operate* through them. During this *step*, the *servant* has learned that God has methods and actions of *affecting* and impacting lives that work—because they are his ways and they always lead to life.

God desires that the *servant seek* him for the next *step* of *servant* growth, which is *teaching*. The *servant* has *celebrated blessing*, and now God wants them to get the *revelation* of the need to *teach*. He will take action to promote that *revelation* in the *servant* and will wait.

Reflections and Discussion

Please reflect on the questions presented in the section titled "Main Discussion Guide for the Servant Process" on page 195. Additionally, the following questions focus on *bless*:

1. What does a *blessing* from God look like?

2. What are some chastisements that are *blessings* from God, and what does it seem that they are meant to accomplish?

Teach

Assertions about the Role of Teach

God *teaches* us that his Word is true and he puts it in our Spirits. In the *role* of *teach* the *servant* encourages the humble *student* to *do* the Word.[327] The Word tells us that righteousness is the act of *believe* in God's truth.[328] When we read about the righteousness of man in the Word of God, the Word comes alive even more when we pronounce it as "*believing* God," because man's *believing* in God is righteousness. In Psalm 23:3 below, read *righteousness* as "*believing* God" and then "*He leads me in paths of righteousness for his name's sake.*" It becomes more alive to understanding as it now reads, "*He leads me in paths of believing him for his name's sake.*"

God provided a *revelation* to me about Psalm 23:[329] a visualization that applies to the *role* of the *teacher*. This Psalm provides examples of our walk from the storms of life to eternal life. In the visualization, we are standing before a level, green, grassy area. To the left, the terrain inclines quickly to become a mountain, where our spiritual walk begins. To the right of the green, grassy area the land slopes down a hill, and the ground gently levels out to a small lake of still water. The lake is directly to our right and down the hill in the level area. A path circles the lake, and many paths lead away from the path that circles the lake. All paths leading away from the lake descend into a deep valley, which is out of sight from where we stand in front of the green, grassy area. We can see in the far distance to the right that a path ascends up out of the valley going up a mountain and out of our sight. We are unable to see that far away clearly. Psalm 23:1-6 describes that as the shepherd, God protects us from the storms of life through eternal life.

Verse 1: "*The LORD is my shepherd, I shall not be in want.*" God is providing and rescuing us from the storms of life.

Verse 2: "*He makes me lie down in green pastures, he leads me beside quiet waters,*" He shows us peace and woos us into safety and restoration.

Verse 3*: "He restores my soul. He guides me in paths of righteousness for his name's sake.*" He shows us his salvation and begins to *teach* by leading us in paths of *believing* him (righteousness) for his name's sake. God will lead us around and around and around that lake in *teach* mode. He is saying, *"I will teach this to you. Believe me, believe me, believe me."* Around and around we go until truth sinks in. Over and over *teach* extols truth that is meant to be planted deep within us to eventually produce good fruit. At the right time, we are steered away from the path around the lake, onto a path headed for the valley, and we enter verse 4.

Verse 4: "*Even though I walk through the valley of the shadow of death, I will fear no evil, for you are with me; your rod and your staff, they comfort me.*" The Father begins to test us, not tempt us.

Remember him saying, "*Believe me, believe me, believe me, believe me*" as we go around the lake? Now he tests, "*Do you believe me?*" Off we go into the valley we could not see from where we originally stood. Off we go, not into death but the illusion of death, where the enemy's lies are heard clearly and they conflict with what God has told us. God's focus is, "*Do you believe me? Will you do what I have taught you?*" He desires to use us but he cannot use us if we do not prove that we *believe*. We must *do* the Word and disregard the lies of the enemy that we are being bombarded with. It becomes clear that we do not respond perfectly every time, when it says, "*Your rod and staff comfort me.*" The rod and staff here can be perceived as guidance, whether it is a Word of encouragement, a reminder of the goal, a correction, or a serious rebuke. We made a mistake, left God's path, and he had to correct us for his glory by calling us back to his path. When God corrects us, his correction is meant to draw us closer to him, not push us away. (The same standard must apply to us as we correct our children.) When we prove that we *believe* him and *do* what he has taught us, we graduate to verse 5.

Verse 5: "*You prepare a table before me in the presence of my enemies. You anoint my head with oil; my cup overflows.*" God prepares a table before us in the very presence of the enemy, not because we are hungry, but because he is *celebrating* our victory of proving to him that we *believe* what he has taught us. The enemy is still standing in our presence saying the same things, but he is defeated because we no longer let his lies affect our actions. We *believe* God and only God. On the table before us is a banquet of truth and *blessings* that we could neither comprehend nor *accept* before this time because we were not ready. Now we are ready. Now we can *receive* and *operate* with truth that *changes* us; truth that supports us on a mission; and truth that, as clean vessels, we use in service to our Father. Truth and *empowerment* from God overflows, we cannot contain it all; our cup overflows in life, ministry, and service. God flows liberally through our lives and we move into verse 6.

Verse 6: "*Surely goodness and love will follow me all the days of my life, and I will dwell in the house of the LORD forever.*" The evidence of the fruit of God in our lives is manifest and exemplified to others as the verse tells us that goodness and mercy follow us all the days of our lives. Eternal life is the end result as we make our way up the path into the mountains that were not very visible, originally, and we dwell in the house of the Lord forever.

Reasons for the Role of Teach

The *teaching role* of the *servant* calls the *student* to begin to walk in the truth, and walk out the truth of God, as revealed in scripture. The *student* has matured through *receiving* and must begin to apply the truth to their lives. God enters the *teaching* mode to move the *student* from *receiving* into *doing*.[330] The *teaching role* exposes the *student* to truth, hoping to draw them into *doing*. Some truth may fall on hearts that are ready, and some may not.[331]

The *revelation* visualization of Psalm 23 is an example of the

Lord working in the *role* of the *teacher*. God always wants his people to be taught, because even the good soil, which is producing one-hundred-fold fruit, needs to be tilled as noted in Proverbs 27:17, which says, *"As iron sharpens iron, so one man sharpens another."* The *teaching role* is vital to this sharpening. The Apostle Paul notes the *role* of the *teacher* as important enough to have special mention as a calling.[332] The *teaching role* can take many forms in various positions. A few will be church pastors, church teachers, Sunday school teachers, and Bible study teachers. Efforts in the *teaching role* allow God[333] to reveal to the *student* what they need to *do*.

Challenge to Accept the Role of Teach

God *equips* the *servant*[334] and still they must *get* and *accept* the *revelation* that they have been *equipped* by God for the role of the *teacher*. The *servant* must *desire* and *invite* that *role* into their lives. While walking out the *role*, the *servant* must *permit* and *embrace* God's *operating* through them and be used to *affect change* in *students*.

Has God moved and *empowered* you through *speaking, caressing, offering,* and *blessing*? Are you sensing God's call to *teach*? Does truth burn in you, and strain to be *shared* in God's way and in God's timing? Do you have a *desire* from God to *teach* and have a crowd of people moved in their spirits with each person thinking you were addressing them personally and awed by truth, which God utters through your lips or hands? The harvest is waiting, but there are few laborers.[335] Allow God to move you into the *teaching role* to draw the *student* to a higher calling.[336] You need not be too concerned, because God will use you as a willing vessel to say[337] what he wants said[338] and the *student* will know that it is God.[339] The *servant* in the *teaching role* will rightly divide truth from deception and steer *students* in all things.[340] Humble power flows through this *servant,* and miracles can be anticipated. Truth is delivered by *teaching* with *speaking, caressing, offering,* and *blessing*. These cumulatively draw the *student* to *doing*.

Incorrect Understanding Of Teach

In Matthew 23:4,[341] Jesus revealed a situation where the religious leaders were missing God. They were sinning, because they were not lifting a finger to *teach* those burdened by a load. Read Matthew 23 to see "*the seven woes,*" where Jesus strongly chastised the teachers of the day for their incorrect teaching of God's children. Until a *servant* has been able to *offer* the gifts of God and *bless* others, they will not *affectively operate* in the role of the *teacher,* because *offering* and *blessing* are "giving away" *roles* and *teaching* is a *role* focused on giving away God's truth. We cannot give away what we do not have. Jesus rebuked the teachers in Matthew 23, because they were not *affectively* giving God away; they were not evidencing *speaking,* *caressing, offering,* and *blessing.*

Beneficiaries of the Role of Teach

The response to the *teaching* of God is for the *student* to begin to *do* the Word.[342] As exemplified in the illumination of Psalm 23, each *student* learns at a different pace, and God patiently takes them around the Lake of Learning, as many times as needed to get the truth deep inside them.[343] God desires the *student* to understand truth so completely that their lives are radically *changed* from the inside out. The *student* may be sent to read the same scripture passage multiple times or be sent on Bible studies that cover the same topic in similar ways. God is *teaching* to get the *student* to *do.*

Resistance to the Benefits of Teach

The Father desires to *teach* always. Jesus Christ did nothing without consulting, honoring, and obeying the Father[344] out of love. A review of the New Testament will show that Jesus approached almost every moment as an opportunity to *teach.* His desire is for the *student* to enter the *doing step* and not stay in the *receiving step.* He will *teach* us until his testing proves that we are in *do* and until the *student* starts walking out his truth as a lifestyle. God will take the *student* around and around that lake in *teaching* mode until the *student* enters the *doing step.* If we see God *teaching* a *student* over and over, expressing the same theme, it may be a signal that they are not walking out what they are being taught. Interesting though, the disciples who spent a lot of time with Jesus had trouble understanding all that Jesus did in the *teaching* mode.[345] An example is

God *sending* a *student* to read James 3 about the tongue being a fire many times over and over. The *student* is not realizing that their tongue is guilty of being the fire. They are not in the *doing mode*, so God continues to *teach* over and over and over in his gentle fashion.

If God is telling a *student* to read the same scripture passage more than once, find out what God is trying to *teach*. There is value for the *student* to focus on the Holy Spirit's directed understanding of that passage, so they can *do* that Word, implementing it into their life. If it takes reading it a dozen times a day for a dozen months, the *student* will grow from that adventure and learn to *do*. God wants the *student* to have illumination from the Spirit on this matter. It is not the words we are to *seek*, but the truth that comes through the words. Do not read the Bible to know the Bible; read the Bible to know the Father. God always wants to *teach* that his Word is true and plant that truth deep into the heart of the *student* to produce good fruit and *glorify* him.

When a *student* is *doing* God's Word, living it out in all facets of their life, this indicates growth, which allows God to move the *student* from *doing* to *caretaking*. To assist the *student*, the *servant* will move from *teaching* to *mending*.

Promotion beyond Teach

Promotion from God will not come until the *servant* gives *glory* to God for being used in the *role*, *celebrates* the growth in the *student*, and *worships* God as the changer. At this time of promotion, the *servant* has learned to *teach* by letting God *operate* through them. During this *step*, the *servant* has learned to communicate to *students* in God's gentle ways, how to do God's Word, and how to walk God's path.

God desires that the *servant seek* him for the next *step* of *servant* growth, which is *mending*. The *servant* has *celebrated teaching*, and now God wants them to get the *revelation* of the need to *mend*. He will take action to promote that *revelation* in the *servant* and will wait.

Reflections and Discussion

Please reflect on the questions presented in the section titled "Main Discussion Guide for the Servant Process" on page 195. Additionally, the following questions focus on *teach*:

1. What does God want the *servant* to communicate in the role of the *teacher*?

2. What is the role of the *teacher* when truth is not being honored?

Mend

Assertions about the Role of Mend

God *mends* the brokenness in our lives and hearts in his time and by his plan. It is by his truth that we are set free. His Word is truth.[346] He *sends* his truth to heal us.[347] In Matthew 13, the Parable of the Sower shows that God is the farmer, who sows the Word into our lives, *seeking* to produce a good crop. The crop is righteousness;[348] *believing* him. He leads us in paths of righteousness to promote the Lordship of Jesus Christ in our lives.

There are different kinds of healing in the Bible: physical and emotional. The physical healing is to open the ears and validate truth to *affect belief.* In John 10:38, Jesus said, *"Even though you do not believe me, believe the miracles"*—the miracles are undeniable signs to cause *belief* of things previously denied. The emotional healing occurs in the *mending step,* where the focus is on a spiritual healing: a healing of the thoughts,[349] a correction of deception, and the casting out of darkness.[350] Perfect truth accomplishes the *mending step.* When the enemy has corrupted our lives or we have not been taught the truth yet, God's truth is the medication needed to *mend* our thought lives and grow spiritually.

Proverbs 14:12 indicates, *"There is a way that seems right to a man, but in the end it leads to death."* During the *mending step,* God develops the *student* to begin to see the truth in that passage and consistently think more like him. In Psalms 23:3,[351] the truth says that *"He leads me in paths of righteousness for his name's sake."* Paraphrased, "He leads us in paths of *believing* him for his name's sake." *Believing* God produces emotional healing.[352] Emotional fractures and brokenness come from the enemy of our souls. *Inviting* God and allowing God to illuminate his unlimited truth into our limited understanding of painful emotional memories and errant conclusions produces a heart cleansed of corruption, death, decay, and bitterness. It is difficult to love someone as God loves them, while still entertaining emotionally wounded memories about them. The truth of God *transforms* us, not because of mandates to *transform*, but as a result of our relationship with the source and author of love.

The enemy comes to kill, steal, and destroy our lives.[353] His ultimate goal is not our flesh, our possessions, or our stable lives, but his goal is to minimize and eliminate our desire and possibilities for turning to God to *seek* his truth. He would rather keep us in constant turmoil by killing, stealing, and destroying things in our lives, and he wants to convince us to blame God for our problems, turn away from God, be too busy to *seek* God, or even *know* to *seek* him. So many of our world's cultures teach us to depend upon anything but God to meet our needs, but God desires to meet all of our needs.[354] Until we allow God to *mend* our emotions and understanding with his truth, we wander through life and life situations. It is this point in our growth, after we repeatedly *do* the Word that the truth begins to *mend* us. There are as many paths of *mend* as there are paths of hurt, deception, misunderstanding, and confusion in the world.

God, who knows us best and most completely and loves us with total devotion, has a plan for *mend* that will take us from just being in the *doing stage* to taking *care* of that truth—protecting it, guarding it, tending it, and allowing its growth in our lives. His *mending step* takes us from just walking out truth by faith, trusting that God is telling the truth and that he knows best, to arrive at that place many describe as, *"I know that I know that I know."* It is like the difference between renting truth and owning truth, between watching a marathon and running a marathon, and between driving the speed limit because you are afraid to get caught speeding and driving the speed limit because it is the right thing to do. It is a shift of perspective. Presented in parable terms, it is the difference between being rocky ground and fertile soil that is being tilled by God to produce good fruit.

The growth that comes from God[355] *mends* our thinking and that produces healing to our souls. Being in the *doing* mode is a good thing, but it too is a *step*. It is a *step* that has a beginning and no ending, and it is a platform on which the next *step* of growth must solidly rest.

Reasons for the Role of Mend

The role of the *mender* is to call the *student* to enter the *caring* mode and get them to tend the Word inside of them. Without *mending*, the *student* stays in a faithful world of *doing*, obediently walking and literally living by the law and seldom seeing the great victories. They quote the victory scriptures in faith, wondering inside why they still feel like the victim. Their mind is still fractured and not yet as focused as God intends them to focus. They have the seed of truth but little growth and victory. The *servant* in the *mending role affectively* moves the *student* from just being in the *doing mode* to being in the *caring step*, a significant *step* of growth. The growth appears as humble maturity, because the *student* is now confident that God is the giver of the seed of truth and the one who matures it as well.

Challenge to Accept the Role of Mend

God *equips* the *servant*,[356] and still they must *get* and *accept* the *revelation* that they have been *equipped* by God for the role of the *mender*. The *servant* must *desire* and *invite* this *role* into their lives. While walking out the *role*, the *servant* must *permit* and *embrace* God *operating* through them, and be used to effect *change* in *students*.

Have you been matured through *speak, caress, offer, bless,* and *teach*? Do you have a burning passion to speak healing into hearts and minds, and a deep *desire* to see others *transformed* by the renewing of their minds? Having learned to *speak, caress, offer, bless,* and finally *teach* the way that God desires you to *teach* by saying everything and only what God wants said in a situation, God could be preparing you to be in the *mending role* to *change* lives. *Servants* who *mend* are in *roles* such as pastor, counselor, bible study leader, recovery group facilitator, mentor, and others whom God has prepared to surround listeners with sweet healing truth. *Servants* who *mend* are stable, with durative unwavering faith because they are certain of God's truth. Their presentation persistently sooths and heals broken hearts. They encourage the *student* to recognize the value of the seed planted, and of repeating the *do* until a *desire* is born to enter the *care step*. Is God calling you to *mend* and help a *student* to *care?* The *mend role* is a vitally important to growth.

Beneficiaries of the Role of Mend

The response to the *mending* of God is for the *student* to *care* for the truth planted inside. God begins *mend* in the life of a *student,* because he sees that they need to go from *doing* to *caring* and be completely *changed* by truth. This is watching, guarding, protecting, and nurturing truth planted in them. As a *servant*, do you find yourself being in front of those who need to be *transformed* by the renewing of their minds? Are they walking out the *doing* and not really having great victories in their lives? These *students* need to be nurtured into *caring* mode. They need the role of the *mender* to be a constant encouragement, so they will jealously guard that truth inside them: to hang on to the truth when the enemy tells them to discard it. *Students* need to live in this mode of *caring.* This is typically a long process of growth, and perhaps they need to be taught the same thing over and over or be sent to the same scriptural truth, until illumination occurs. They need to not just allow truth to *change* them; they need to *invite* that *change* and pursue that *change.*

Our Redeemer lives and died to allow truth to *change* us. We are the victor and not the victim. His desire is to *mend* our brokenness,[357] heal the hurts brought on by the enemy, and launch us into the victorious life that Jesus shed his blood for. God wants us back. He wants the truth to *transform* us. He wants to *transform* us by the renewing of our minds. He wants us to jealously guard the truth within us and be *caretakers of* the truth planted in our spirits.

Resistance to the Benefits of Mend

As a *servant*, we may see God putting a *student* on the shelf, seemingly to just walk out the truth and nothing else. This could be a signal that God is in the *mending* mode, because the *student* needs to *care* for the truth planted inside of them. If there is no "working on self" or letting God work[358] on them to purify and perfect their faith, they may be stuck in this *step* of *mending* and *caring*. They will be stuck until they guard the truth planted in them and allow God to move them to the next level in maturity.[359] God continues to *mend,* until the *student* gets into *care* and is *transformed.* God continues to attempt to *mend* our lives, but when we are unfertile soil, the hard times cause the seed to be spiritually ineffective. An example of not being in the *caring* mode and not being *transformed* by the renewing of their minds is the nation of Israel on the way to the promised land in Deuteronomy 1–2. Because they did not grow as they needed, they were allowed to wander through the desert for forty years, until they were *transformed* by *caring* mode and were walking out truth.

There are broken hearts, which resist the *mending* influence and resist entering the *caring step.* In the Parable of the Sower in Mark 4:13–20,[360] these resistant hearts are rocky soil and the ground with thorns. Massive numbers of growth-starved Christians are stuck here, not allowing the Word to *transform* them, merely playing at Christianity, and acting like members of a social club instead of standing victorious as children of the living God. Lacking *empowered* teachers or open hearts, they wander through life, ignorant and unaware and then perish without actually being *transformed.*[361]

As the *student* enters *care* and allows a *transforming* of their minds,[362] God moves from the *mending role* to the *empowering role* to move the *student* from *caring* into *showing.*

Promotion beyond Mend

Promotion from God will not come until the *servant* gives *glory* to God for being used in the *role, celebrates* the growth in the *student,* and *worships* God as the changer. At this time of promotion, the *servant* has learned to *mend* by letting God *operate* through them.

During this *step*, the *servant* has learned to communicate to *students* in God's gentle ways, how to protect the gem of truth, and how to allow God's truth to *transform* their thinking, resulting in significantly *transformed* lives.

God desires that the *servant seek* him for the next *step* of *servant* growth, which is *empowerment*. The *servant* has *celebrated mending*, and now God wants them to get the *revelation* of the need to *empower*. He will take action to promote that *revelation* in the *servant* and will wait.

Reflections and Discussion

Please reflect on the questions presented in the section titled "Main Discussion Guide for the Servant Process" on page 195. Additionally, the following questions focus on *mend*:

1. How does the *mend* role *affect student* lives?

2. Explain why this book could be *operating* in the role of *mend*.

Empower

Assertions about the Role of Empower

God always *empowers* his Word. God is the power behind his Word and his truth. In Isaiah 55:8–11,[363] God demonstrates the massive difference between his thoughts and our thoughts. He declares that he has the power to cause things to happen and that his Word is alive and full of life. His Word always accomplishes what he wants it to accomplish. His power is behind his Word. His power is behind his promises. He *empowers* his Word and *empowers* his promises. He *empowers* those he prepares.[364] He *empowers* those who are humble and not just *believe* that he is the source of all things but who walk out that understanding. Pride lives in "*I do,*" but humility lives in, "*He does*[365] *through me.*" *Empower* lives in humility, which walks out his Lordship in our lives. Wisdom builds humility,[366] and humility builds *empowerment.* Without humility, there can be no *empowerment.*

Empowerment from God occurs to let the Holy Spirit of Truth[367] *transform* the life of the *student.*[368] As the attraction of and the yielding to sin diminishes in the *student's* life, the power of God comes with authority.[369] His victory over the influence of the enemy in their lives allows them to walk in humble, graceful holiness. God *empowers* the *student* to walk in this holiness,[370] which is him flowing freely through them. While much of the function of *empower-*

ment is accomplished by God, he does use *servants* moved by God in efforts that include promotion and recognition of the *student*. Promotion may manifest as more exposure in public arenas to allow the *student* to touch more lives. *Empowerment* will produce fruit based on the same truth that set the *student* free.[371]

Reasons for the Role of Empower

The *empowering role* recognizes and rewards maturity in the *student* by encouraging them to display evidences that God is the source of all things in his life.

The *student* is maturing past the *caring* mode, because they have successfully tended truth, let it grow in their life, and are consistently walking out the Word. The *student* has learned to trust, honor, and obey at a level that was not comprehendible during earlier days of the walk. Given a choice today, they repeatedly *seek* and choose the path of godliness, holiness, and righteousness. God now has a vessel that moves when he tells them to move and does what God wants done. The *student* has learned to let go and let God. They have a smooth yet very real transition ahead of them. The *student* is ready for God to *empower*. Using the role of the *empowerer*, God will mature the *student* from *caring* to *showing*, and by silent examples, others will know that the *student* is *transformed* by the renewing of their mind. When leadership *empowers* someone, they are given the resources to accomplish an objective. In the same way, when God enters *empower* mode to move on a *student*, he desires to give them the resources to accomplish his will, to walk out his way, and be a vessel to let his Word accomplish that for which it was sent. The Holy Spirit has a home, is welcomed, and is *invited*. The Holy Spirit wants to put a sign out in front of the *student* that says, "*God lives in here. Watch this person to see the proof.*" The *role* of the *empowerer* posts that sign, allowing the fruit of the Spirit[372] to become evident. The *student*, by living in the *caring* mode, has let God sweep and clean the temple, and the Holy Spirit is moving in and erecting a large, obvious billboard out front. In a crisis situation, the *student* can praise God in all things, not because of a crisis, but because they are comfortable that God's billboard is out front lit up brightly,[373] and he is preparing the *student* to *show* his glory throughout the event.

Challenge to Accept the Role of Empower

God *equips* the *servant*[374] and still they must *get* and *accept* the *revelation* that they have been *equipped* by God for the *role* of the *empowerer*. The *servant* must *desire* and *invite* that *role* into their lives. While walking out the *role*, the *servant* must *permit* and *embrace* God *operating* through them and be used to *affect change* in *students*.

Has God matured you through *speak, caress, offer, bless, teach,* and *mend*? Has God put you in an administrative *role* with discernment and ability to promote and recognize others? Do you have a *desire* in your heart, which is put there by God to *empower* other believers? Do you have gifts from God that move people to a more mature walk and to cause people to be bold in their faith with a boldness centered on faith in God's truth? When you encourage others, do reports return to you about fruit from that encouragement that exhibits the presence of God? God has to mature us to enter and *accept* the role of the *empowerer*, and he does it to cause *students* to openly and silently exhibit the presence of God in their lives. A *servant* in this *role* will also *empower* by encouragement.

God will not *empower* those who do not know him or know his Word[375] and truth.[376] To enter this *role*, study and know truth.[377]

Beneficiaries of the Role of Empower

The response to the *empowerment* of God is for the *student* to *show* that their heavenly Father is Lord in their life. Observers know without asking. *Students* will move from the *step* of *caring* to the *step* of *showing*—from closely guarding that seed of truth and allowing God to nurture its growth to silently evidencing that their lives are good ground and that the seed of truth has been planted, nurtured, and now blossoming. The fruit is maturing and looks like a crop that will produce great results. A word to the underground churches: when God *empowers* the *student*, underground and hidden churches can flourish, because no one has to question whether someone is a believer. It just *shows* silently. Your church will grow due to this.

Resistance to the Benefits of Empower

Some *students* do not exhibit that God is their Lord. God desires that we *show* by silent example that we have the light of Christ in us. By the time the *student* grows through the *step* of *caring*, there is a firm belief being walked out and lived out in the life of the believer. Progression to the next *step* of *showing* would seem to be a given, but the enemy of our souls is crafty and will have some lives resistant to entering the *step* of *showing*. Getting the *student* to resist the *step* of *showing* is a significant victory for the enemy. If this corrupted victory is realized, the *student* will have a salvation experience and a Lordship experience with the Father, but the experience will *affect* no one else, because there will be no evidence of the work that God has accomplished.

This lack of *showing* is seen in some *students* who have been taught by the enemy through their culture and family that faith is a private thing and should not be *shared*. Churches can die due to this infection of deception, because there will be no growth, no outreach, no evangelism, and no mission work. These *students* are stuck in the *caring step*, because their lives are *changed* and they are good people, but there is no evidence of Christianity showing in their lives; no visible billboard erected by the Holy Spirit. This is in direct opposition to the Great Commission delivered by God the Father through Jesus Christ.[378]

Consider an example of a *student* who has meditated on the Word and has sincerely humbled themselves before him, being *transformed* from the inside out, but no evidence is obvious. Perhaps they are shy or have some other personality issue or wound, but there does not seem to be fruit of the Holy Spirit. God's Holy Spirit will continue to *empower* that person to eventually *show* by silent example that the person has been renewed—to allow the billboard of the Holy Spirit to *show*. The Holy Spirit will work to overcome negative events or negative attitudes that conflict with his perfect will and desire for us. He wants to manifest the fruit of the Spirit, and it is the power of and presence of God within us that *affects* this.

Our heavenly Father desires everyone to mature into and

through this *step* of growth. In Galatians 5:22–23, the scripture says there is no law against this fruit being evident in our lives. The enemy would convince some that this relationship with God needs to be kept secret, but God would have this evidence clearly displayed to all without talking or preaching. God will use the *servant* in this *role* to encourage the *student*.

As a *servant*, have you encountered *students* stuck in *care* who have not progressed to *show*? If the *student* remains in *caring mode*, God will continue to *empower* them to move them to the *showing step*. God will continue to illuminate that billboard planted out in front of the *student*, desiring that it *show*.

God *empowers* us by filling us with his Spirit and gives us boldness in him to accomplish his mission in our lives. The response to God *empowering* is for the *student* to *show*.

Promotion beyond Empower

Promotion from God will not come until the *servant* gives *glory* to God for being used in the *role*, *celebrates* the growth in the *student*, and *worships* God as the changer. At this time of promotion, the *servant* has learned to *empower* by letting God *operate* through them. During this *step,* the *servant* has learned to *affect students* in God's excellent ways—resulting in those around the *student* observing a significantly *transformed* life.

God desires that the *servant seek* him for the next *step* of *servant* growth, which is to *send*. The *servant* has *celebrated empowerment*, and now God wants them to get the *revelation* of the need to *send*. He will take action to promote that *revelation* in the *servant* and will wait.

Reflections and Discussion

Please reflect on the questions presented in the section titled "Main Discussion Guide for the Servant Process" on page 195. Additionally, the following questions focus on *empower*:

1. What would it look like for you to *empower* someone?

2. What role does encouragement play in this *role* of *empowerment*?

Send

Assertions About The Role of Send

God always *sends* us[379] where we cannot go ourselves, so he can *show* himself as the source and strength,[380] and to make it clear that he is the one who *empowers* and *sends*.[381] Jesus *sent* the twelve disciples to drive out evil spirits and heal the sick in Matthew 10:1.[382] Through Jesus, the Father charged them with something they could not accomplish by themselves, except as evidence that he is the one who *empowers*, he is the one who *sends*,[383] and he is the source.

The Great Commission is found in Matthew 28:18–20:

> *Then Jesus came to them and said,*
> *All authority in heaven and on earth has been given to me. Therefore*
> *go and make disciples of all nations, baptizing them in the name of*
> *the Father and of the Son and of the Holy Spirit, and teaching them*
> *to obey everything I have commanded you. And surely I am with you*
> *always, to the very end of the age.*

As Jesus Christ *speaks* these Words, he is in *send* mode. Three important statements are made by Jesus: (1) I have authority to do this, (2) Go, and (3) I am with you. Note that he did not *send* them out *unequipped*, and he did not *send* out brand new believers. He *sent* out those he had already prepared.

When we make the choice to go without being *sent*, we become like Sarai and Abram (read Genesis 16) birthing Ishmaels that plague generations with fruit from bad choices, originating with us at the top of the family tree as we birth wild donkeys.[384] When we take a God idea and implement it in man's timing, we will not have God's results.[385] We have man's results, which will eventually yield a wild donkey. Proverbs 16:25 makes it clear, *"There is a way that seems right to a man, but its end is death."* All works initiated by man and flesh produce death of one kind or another, because the motive is not purely eternal.

Our Father further clarifies the differences in motive and results, when he says in Isaiah 55:9–11:

> *As the heavens are higher than the earth, so are my ways higher than your ways and my thoughts than your thoughts. My word that goes out from my mouth will not return to me empty, but will accomplish what I desire and achieve the purpose for which I sent it.*

God is making it clear that when he *sends* us for his purpose, it will accomplish his mission. In John 21:6 it says, *"He said, 'Throw your net on the right side of the boat and you will find some.' When they did, they were unable to haul the net in because of the large number of fish."* This is where Jesus sent the empty handed fisherman back to fish, and the results were wonderful.

Observe Jesus, as he went where he was *sent*. There are many examples, yet focusing on just one pair, we see Jesus in Mark 5:25–29,[386] where the woman with an issue of blood for twelve years touched Jesus without his prior awareness. Power went out of him and healed her. Power was there, because he was prepared and *sent* by the Father. Later, he touched a little dead girl and commanded life back into her.[387] Power from the Father flowed through him and *affected* a miracle. No Ishmaels were birthed there, because Jesus Christ waited to for God to *send*.

Reasons for the Role of Send

How can someone *hear* unless there is a *speaking*, and how can someone *speak* unless there is a *sending*?[388] God must *send* in order for fruitful activities to be the result. We must wait for God to *send* us, if we are to produce his fruit.[389] Man cannot *send* out of his own heart and devices. If we settle for anything less than a God *send,* we stand prepared to birth Ishmaels as exemplified in Genesis 16. In Matthew 9:38, where Jesus said, *"Ask the Lord of the harvest, therefore, to send out workers into his harvest field,"* he did not say, *"Just get out there, and speak the gospel to people."* He instructed us to *ask* God to *send* us. God knows when we are prepared vessels, *equipped* for his glory and honor. A God *send* produces a God-ordained mission.

Challenge to Accept the Role of Send

God *equips* the *servant*[390] and still they must *get* and *accept* the *revelation* that they have been *equipped* by God for the *role* of the *sender.* The *servant* must *desire* and *invite* that *role* into their lives. While walking out the *role,* the *servant* must *permit* and *embrace* God's *operating* through them and be used to effect *change* in *students.*

Has God caused your growth through *speaking, caressing, offering, blessing, teaching, mending,* and *empowering?* Do you have a *desire* in your heart, put there by God, to *send* out prepared believers? Do you have gifts and callings, power and authority from God to commission others for a mission from the Father? Will you allow God to use you to *send* out those who can *show* that the Spirit of God lives in them so that they can *share?* Allow God to use you to *send* them out to serve in humble power and authority just as Jesus sent out his disciples with authority in the Great Commission.[391]

Challenge To Send

If God has *equipped* you, the *servant,* with the authority and provision of what is needed by the *student* as they are *sent,* consider *accepting* the challenge to *send.* Allow God to use you to commission and *send.* This *role* will include activities of an apostle, church starter, and *servant* in leadership *equipped* by God to commission missionaries into the field. These can *accept* the challenge to *send.* The mission field can be the local church and service there or remote areas, but their *role* and call of God are to *send.*

God has matured the *servant,* and he is exhibiting the gifts of the Holy Spirit. He has tested them and found them faithful in little and in much. He has work for them to accomplish, and workers are needed in the harvest fields. He has a place to serve already picked out for the workers and workers picked out to *send*. Accept the *role* and challenge of listening to God and issuing the *send* to spread the gospel to areas remote from yourself, remote from your calling, and perhaps remote from your own mission.[392] As you listen to God for direction to *send*, his purposes will be accomplished. The results will be his, because results come from his Word in his time in his way for his reason and his glory. *Accept* the *servant role* to *send*.

Beneficiaries of the Role of Send

The response to God *sending* is for the *student* to *share*. Being *sent* by God, the *student* manifests a deep *desire* to *share* what they have been taught, because it is a fire burning in the heart, a truth that must be let out, and a spark that must be communicated, hoping to ignite another soul to see the truth that *transforms*. In the Great Commission, Jesus tells the mature to go into the whole world and preach. That is a *send*, so go and *share*.

Nearly anyone can participate in a mission trip to serve God, and though the *sender* desires to *send* godly *servants*, it is possible to have participants who are not as prepared as a *sender* would desire. Recipients of a mission trip may notice that some participants do not have the first commandment fully functional in their lives, but when God *sends*, he will still shine through the mission effort as a whole and be glorified.

If the prepared *student* declines the *send*, God will *send* again and again, until the *student* honors him and responds. God so greatly desires laborers in the field that, in the biblical book of Jonah, he arranged a special ride to the mission field, because he saw the mission so important. Many *sent* by God into the mission field would certainly confirm that each *send* by God is one of the best experiences of their lives, because it is awesome and full of wonder.

Resistance to the Benefits of Send

Some *students* resist sharing what God has taught them. God desires that we *share* what we have been taught. The *student* has been prepared and is *showing* evidence of God's Lordship in their lives. The *student's* next growth is to *share*. If he declines the call of *sending*, God will *send* again when the *student* is ready to honor him and to respond. Progression into the *step* of *share* would seem, at this place of maturity to be nearly a given, but we do have a crafty enemy who comes to steal, kill, and destroy.[393]

Marriage and children can change ministry focus for a couple.[394] Marriage tension and discord will certainly allow the enemy to distract a *servant* from their commissioning to go into an external mission. The marriage and the offspring of that marriage are the first mission field—this properly honors God, since the purpose of marriage is to produce godly offspring.[395] A marriage being attacked by the enemy will certainly be and probably should be resistant to the *send* to *share*. If the *servant* is listening to God in this case, the *send* will be either postponed or not occur. Family is the first mission field. This is an accurate example of a *send* with someone being too busy or distracted to honor a *send* and exhibiting a resistance to the call to *share* for a time. God will wait for the right time, and then *send* again, because his gifts and callings are without repentance;[396] he is not sorry that he gifted us, or for his *send* that will use his gifts.

Promotion beyond Send

Promotion from God will not come until the *servant* gives *glory* to God for being used in the *role*, *celebrates* the growth in the *student*, and *worships* God as the changer. By this time in growth, the *servant* has a firm foundation to stand on, a rich-experience base to draw on, and many occasions when God has confirmed that he is the source and power behind the second commandment to give his love away.

God desires that the *servant seek* him for the next *step* of *servant* growth, which will be a more significant level of service. The *servant* has *celebrated sending*, and now God wants them to get the *revelation* of the need for the more significant level of service. He will take action to promote that *revelation* in the *servant* and will wait.

God has no limit or end of service to him, and he will use his *equipped*, prepared, matured, and ready *servant*. The growing *servant* knows that God has no limits and that each new mission stretches their abilities, because the fields need harvesting and no field is the same. Each new mission requires focused prayer and additional faith, resulting in spiritual growth and a deeper relationship with their heavenly Father. An example is in Joshua 13:1, where after a lifetime of conquering lands by the command of God, God says to Joshua, *"You are very old, and there are still very large areas of land to be taken over."* Thankfully, God is never done with our growth.

Reflections and Discussion

Please reflect on the questions presented in the section titled "Main Discussion Guide for the Servant Process" on page 195. Additionally, the following questions focus on *send*:

1. What statements will be made by a *servant* in the *send* role?

2. What activities will be performed by a *servant* in the *send* role?

Expanding the Servant Process

Prior to reading this section, it may be valuable to have a basic understanding of the *steps* and flow of the *Servant Process*. This section expands each *servant step* into more detailed components and presents diagrams to visualize the expansion. Similar to the *student step*, every *step* in the *servant process* has three *seasons*: *preparation*, *operation*, and *celebration*.

Every *step* of *servant-hood* begins with *preparation*, which is training for the new *role*. To accomplish this, the Father *sends* the *servant* through the *student process* to be *transformed* and ready to serve. His desire is to *teach* the *servant* to learn how to not just walk out the *role*, but walk out the *role* like God wants it walked out. Following that *preparation*, the Father wants the *servant* to *operate* in that *role* and be *affectively* used to reach *students*. *Celebration* indicates a readiness to be promoted beyond that *role*.

Every *step* in the *servant process* begins with the *preparation season* followed by the *operation season* and matures into a *celebration season*. This is detailed in outline form below.

1. *Preparation Season* — Letting God prepare and call the *servant*

- Equipping — Submit to being a *student* and being taught through all eight *step*s of the *student process* to learn how God wants the *servant* to function in this new *servant role*. For example: the *caressing step*

- Revelation — That God has *equipped* and called the *servant* for the *role*

- Accept — That God has equipped and called the *servant* for the *role*

- Desire — To let God walk out that *role* through the *servant*

- Invite — To let God walk out that *role* through the *servant*

Note: God will not move a *servant* into the *operation season* unless the *servant* invites. The *invitation* permits God to open the door and the *operation season* can begin.

2. *Operation Season* — Letting God walk out the *role* through the *servant*

- Permit — God's *role*

- Embrace — God's *role*

- Operate — In faith, by letting God walk out the *role* through them, even before *students* are involved

- Affect — Growth in *students* while operating in the *role*

3. *Celebration Season*   Honoring the *operation* of the *role*

- Glorify   God for being used in the *role* to *change students*
- Celebrate   The *changes* in *students* produced by *operating* in the *role*
- Worship   God as the changer
- Seek   God for more *servant* growth

The target is not the *operation season*, the target is the *celebration season*. *Celebration* is about the *role* working and the *student* being *changed*. Humility in the c*elebration season* is *celebration* for being used and *celebration* for *change* produced by the *role* but never *celebration* of the *servant* or the *role*. The humble *servant* will *celebrate* being used as a teacher and not *celebrate* being a teacher. For the *servant*, the focus is not on the *servant* but on God and on the *student* being *changed*. Gift and *role* exaltation can impede promotion of the *servant* to the next *step*.

Enlarging the vision of this *expanded servant process* to additional life roles assigned by God might include service in areas such as frustrating jobs, tough parenting, tough re-parenting, submission to tyrannical authority, and many other focuses that might, at some point, seem less than desirable because the *servant* is expose to less than interested students. In these situations, some may find themselves depleted of energy or motivation. Maturity is found not in the *operation season* but when one arrives at the *Celebration Season* to not just walk out the *role* but *celebrate* being used by God in the *role*. The *role* of the *servant* does not change when the audience fails to respond.

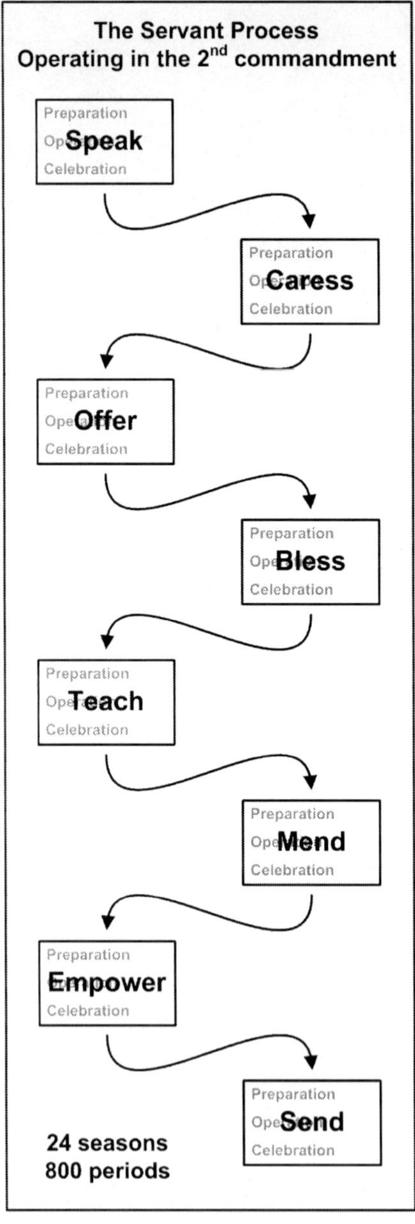

The Expanded Servant Step: 3 Seasons & 100 Periods

Preparation from God

88. Equipping — God's growth through the 88 Periods of the Student Process to learn this walk / role

1. Revelation — Of the call of God
2. Accept — The call of God
3. Desire — The call of God
4. Invite — The call of God

Operation being used by God

5. Permit — God's role
6. Embrace — God's role
7. Operate — In God's role by faith
8. Affect — God's growth in Students

Celebration honoring change

9. Glorify — God for being used
10. Celebrate — God's change in the student
11. Worship — God as the changer
12. Seek — God for more of his growth

The table above is abbreviated for simplicity and shown below.

The first growth step of SPEAK is at top left.

Diagram 7—The Expanded Servant Process
Each of the eight steps include the three seasons:
Preparation, Operation, and Celebration.
The first commandment must be lived out before one is eligible to be a servant.
Copyright 2010 Michael Marburger

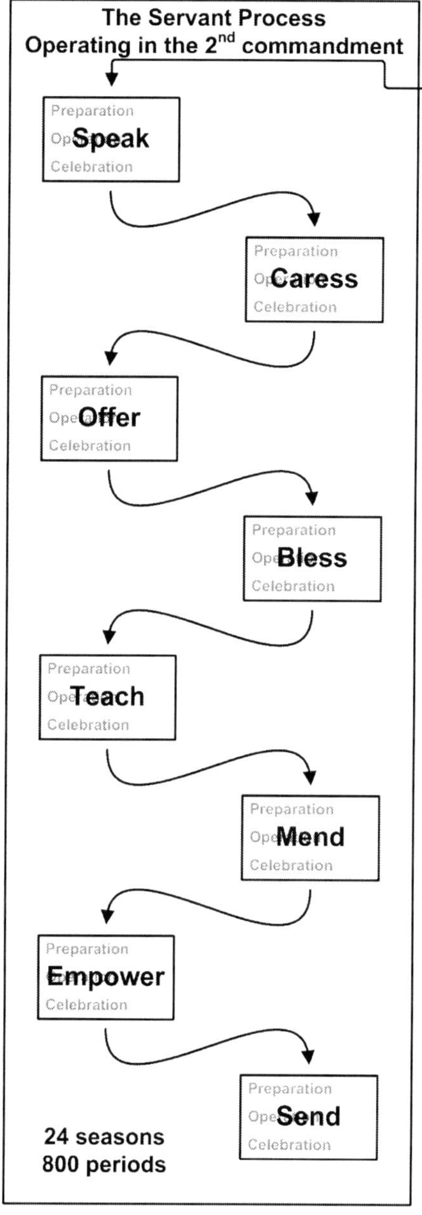

24 seasons / 88 periods

The first commandment must be lived out before God promotes someone to servant.

To learn to operate in a servant role, the servant goes through the Student Process as part of their Preparation Season.

Detailing Growth

The table below presents the reader with a count of the number of periods of growth that must be completed for maturity. This is presented to display the complexity of growth required to be maturing through the various steps.

8	*steps* in the *student process*
11	periods in each of the eight *steps*
88	periods of growth in the *student process* before the first commandment is fully addressed
100	periods in each *step* of the *servant process* (twelve plus the eighty-eight *equipping* periods)
188	periods of growth to get saved, then become trained in the *speaking role*
288	periods of growth to get saved and mature through the *caressing role*
888	periods of growth to get saved and mature through the *sending role*

In Diagram 8, notice the wrap around from *student* to *servant* in Romans 10:14–15,[397] parenthesized for emphasis: *how can they believe in the one of whom they have not heard?* (The first two *student steps*). *And how can they hear without someone preaching to them?* (The first step in *student process* and the *servant process*.) *And how can they preach unless they are sent?* (The first and last *steps* of the *servant process*.)

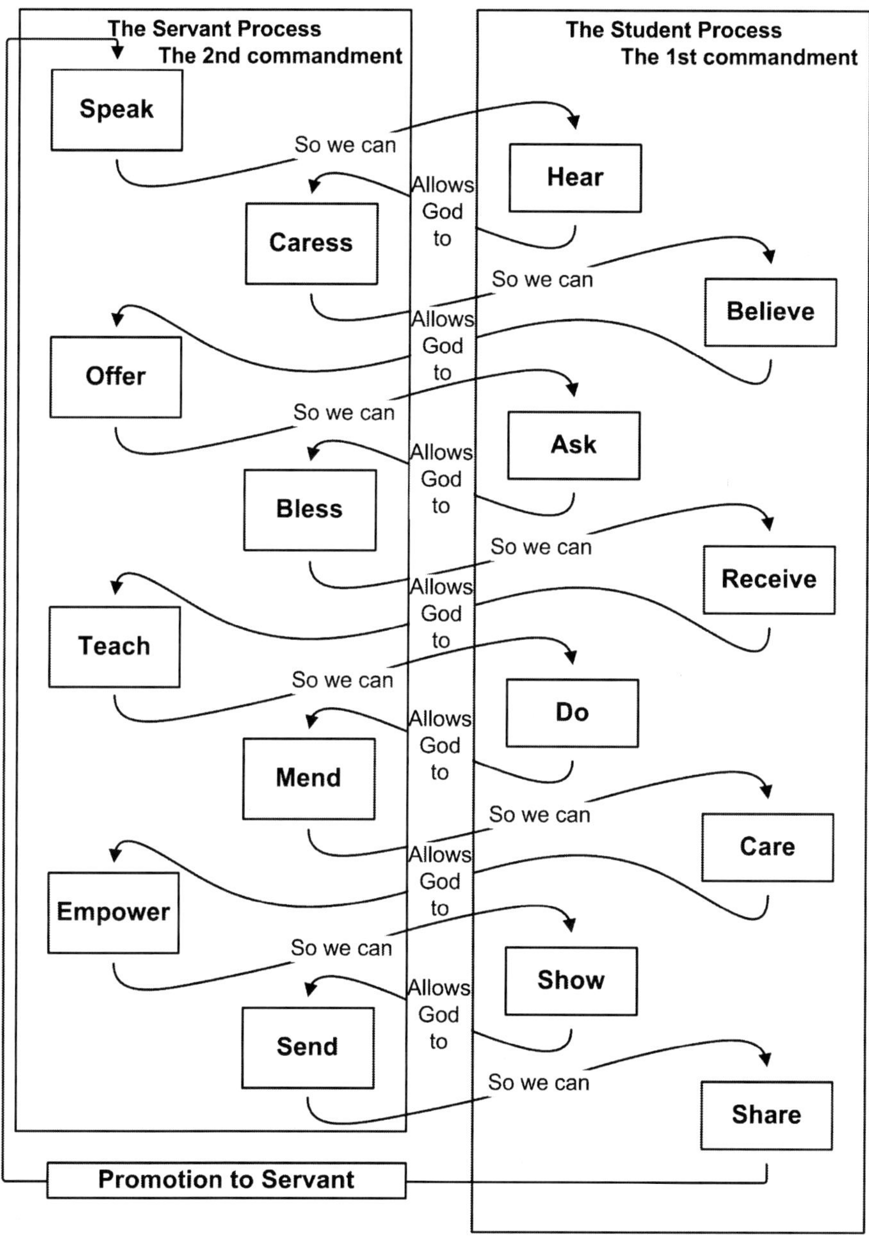

Diagram 8—The Speak to Share Method
The interaction between God (or his servants) and the student, to cause growth.
The role of the servant is to operate in the Great Commission to build disciples.
Students grow into servants (disciples.)   Copyright 2010 Michael Marburger
The Servant Process
The 2nd commandment
The Student Process
The 1st commandment
Speak
So we can
Allows God to
Hear
Caress
So we can
Allows God to
Believe
Offer
So we can
Allows God to
Ask
Bless
So we can
Allows God to
Receive
Teach
So we can
Allows God to
Do
Mend
So we can
Allows God to
Care
Empower
So we can
Allows God to
Show
Send
So we can
Allows God to
Share
Promotion to Servant

The Deception Process

This chapter uses the method similar to the "Speak To Share Method" presented on page 195 to present a method Satan uses to corrupt lives. The life of the student is assaulted by confusing, bruising, twisting, bending, and crippling. Does the fruit of that effort that sound like anyone you have ever met? There is a significant difference between the path God desires for us and the path that Satan, the enemy of our lives, plans for us.

Note that the response of man in this deception-influenced method is somewhat similar to the response of man according to truth-influenced method. The student is exposed to deception from the enemy, which is corruption of God's perfection. They still hear, believe, ask, and receive, and then do by walking according to that corrupted understanding. The result is despair that shows and is shared. They graduate to speaking it out publicly and become a vessel of corruption themselves, as they spread their infection of deception.

Those being called to the Great Commission might benefit from taking note—this is the type of person you are likely to encounter in the missions God sets before you. Your target audience and your mission may be a person whom God loves, yet they are living a life corrupted by the practices of the enemy. The most important issue is not their physical condition in life, but whether they are hearing and receiving truth that sets them free.

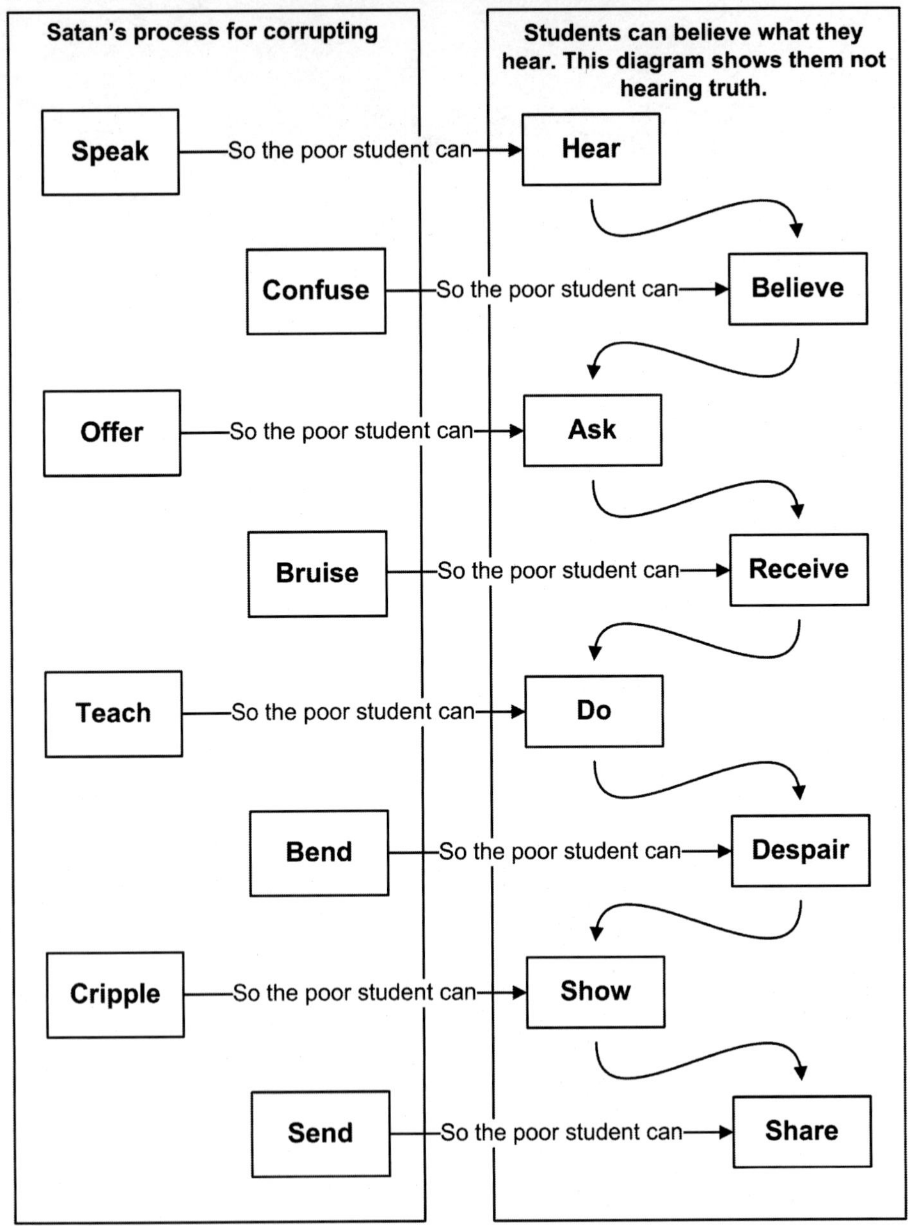

Diagram 9—Satan Corrupting the Student
The enemy corrupts the student through his methods.
Listening to Satan, the student walks a path of destruction.
Copyright 2010 Michael Marburger
Satan's process for corrupting
Students can believe what they hear. This diagram shows them not hearing truth.
Speak
So the poor student can
Hear
Confuse
So the poor student can
Believe
Offer
So the poor student can
Ask
Bruise
So the poor student can
Receive
Teach
So the poor student can
Do
Bend
So the poor student can
Despair
Cripple
So the poor student can
Show
Send
So the poor student can
Share

Expanding the Deception Process

Prior to reading this section, it may be valuable to have a basic understanding of the steps and flow of the "Speak To Share Method" on page 179, as well as "Diagram 9—Satan Corrupting the Student."

Similar to the steps of the student and servant, the steps of the deception process can be expanded. The expanded student step of being corrupted by Satan is below:

1. Recognition Season	Unhealthy conclusions about meeting a need
• Feel a need	Legitimate spiritual need caused by man's built in desire to be in fellowship with the Creator
• Realization	Unspiritual revelation that a medication is available for this pain—this is not a revelation from God[398]
• Acceptance	This medication is available; therefore, it must work

2. Medication Season   Unhealthy changes to meet a need

- Permit   Ungodly wisdom and direction into a life
- Embrace   Repetition breeds contentment in the wrong path
- Transform   Be changed by the deception—stray farther from God

3. Toleration Season   Unhealthy acceptance of an unhealthy situation

- Contentment   With the new change—there is a way that seems right to a man, but its end is death[399]
- Stumble on   Press on, ignorant that the change just made was not from God

As the infection matures and the student becomes the servant, the infector spreads his spiritual disease; the infected becomes the infector. Satan is patient zero for the toxic and fatal infection of deception. His infection spreads life a fire that is never quenched.[400]

Expanded servant step being used by Satan. Hurting people hurt people.

1. Infestation Season   Toxic lifestyle lived in ignorance

- Broken   Spiritually toxic infected with deception and the appearance of wisdom without godly substance
- Ignorant   Spiritually unaware of their toxic condition
- Available   To be able to pass on the toxic deception

2. Distribution Season	Spreading deception practices
• Permit	Actions and interactions that spread the disease
• Embrace	Repetition breeds contentment in the wrong path and corruption of students
• Distribute	Infect students with spiritual deception
3. Denigration Season	Standing in unhealthy judgment of those infected
• Unawareness	Unaware of being used to spiritually infect others, they remain ignorant of their infestation—they perish for lack of knowledge[401]
• Disdain	Private or public dissatisfaction about the situation of the student—Satan attacks us and then insults us, because we have been attacked
• Stumble on	Press on, spiritually empty

The only effective remedy for this infection is found in the Great Commission. Only as *equipped* and called servants of the most high God can we let God *operate* through us to be an *affective servant* to *speak, caress, offer, bless, teach, mend, empower,* and *send.*

The Challenge of the Great Commission

The Great Commission is to build disciples. Disciples are *servants*. As *servants* walking out the Great Commission, we are to build *servants*, not just *students* and not mere *believers*. Building mere *believers* leaves the person woefully short of a mature *student* and seriously short of being *transformed* by the renewing of their mind in the *care step*. Building *students* causes them to be complete in their understanding of the first commandment, but short of maturing into *servants* where they are called to walk out the second commandment. As *servants*, we are commanded to fulfill the Great Commission, birthing and growing additional solid *servants*. Christians who have an eternal relationship with their heavenly Father will repeat this method to bring others into the kingdom of God, teaching them to repeat this method as well.

The method described in "From Speak to Share: How God Builds a Christian" can be used by those walking out the Great Commission to walk it out with the wisdom and effectiveness desired by God in these last days.

Reflections and Discussion

1. Compare being called to make everyone believe and being called to expose everyone to the truth of Christ. Compare "making disciples" and "building Christians."

2. How can we make anything happen? (See Psalm 127:1)

3. How does God want you to *change* to *accept* the challenge of the Great Commission?

4. How has an understanding of these processes *changed* your thinking about witnessing to others about Jesus Christ and being used to help their growth?

5. In your walk with God, where are you in these processes?

God gave the poem below directly to me by *revelation*. It presents God *speaking* to a *servant* who apparently did not go, or it represents God *speaking* to some reader who is resisting the call to go and in doing so resists fulfilling the Great Commission. Read and be blessed, motivated, energized, and ignited.

When I Call

We each stand alone at the foot of the throne
And bow before God we will.
As creation worships the Father of all,
Each one hears, "Peace, be still.

I have a wounded heart right here,
I have a wounded soul.
I know his desire was to do my will,
Yet he was deceived and did not know.

Who was it that I sent to him?
Who was it to whom I said, 'Go?'
What truth did I want him to hear?
And what truth to him did not flow?

I sent you to him, and you know who you are.
I sent you to plant my seed.
I sent you, and you did not go,
And through you, I did not meet his need.

Wander he did, each day and night,
Searching for what was right,
Looking and seeking and asking around,
Overwhelmed in his spiritual fight.

I had a victory planned for him,
A victory he could have won,
A victory to touch many lives,
If you had only gone.

What excuse will you give to me?
What price was way too much?
Since I am the provider of all,
Why did you ignore my touch?

I prompted you and touched you too,
I prepared you for what was to come.
You asked to help, then turned to run,
And did not share my son.

I waited and called and waited again,
And often you came to me in prayer
Asking to be used and seeking my face,
Yet when I called, you acted impaired.

I want you to act; I want you to go.
When I call, I want you to run.
I reach you and teach you and prepare you for use,
And you are ready for this mission of one.

When you go, victories will be won,
    and lives will be changed,
Because you are going for me.
You will speak my Words and do my will,
And the enemy of life will flee.

Turn your heart toward listening,
    your feet toward obedience,
And we will see victories.
Their celebration will be at the foot of the throne,
As my creation looks and sees."

Closing Statement

Remember the thief on the cross who *believed* Jesus? Jesus said in Luke 23:43,[402] "*I tell you the truth, today you will be with me in paradise.*" Clearly, the thief is in heaven and is spending an eternity with the Father. The thief had no time to allow Jesus to be Lord through his life; no time to allow himself to be *transformed* by the renewing of his mind, and no time to bring others to the Father by going into the world and evangelizing. He had fire insurance only. He was snatched from the claws of the enemy just prior to death. He did not have time to *show* someone his faith by his works.[403] He is in heaven, but what size is his reward or crown?[404] Using what God has shown in this book, it might be acceptable to put forth that the Father could welcome the thief into heaven with, "*Welcome home, my son, my student,*" instead of, "my servant,"[405] because he *showed* an awareness of his heavenly Father, and that Jesus had the power to deliver him to heaven. But because he confessed that he was getting what his deeds deserved, he was clearly not living a *transformed* life. He was still working on getting the first commandment worked out; he was not a *servant* of God.

Throughout the New Testament, we read letters from *servants* like Paul who did many acts of service for the Father. A life of service is what God desires. Paul clarifies this by writing in Philippians 1:21, "*For to me, to live is Christ and to die is gain.*" When we have lived a life allowing Jesus to be Lord through us, our heavenly Father is pleased. We long to hear one day, our heavenly Father say the sweetest words we can imagine, "*Welcome home good and faithful servant.*" All growth springs from a God Word for a God reason in a God way and a God time for God's glory. You are encouraged to allow yourself to be the *student* in all areas of life, be grown into a *servant* in all areas of life, and live a life dedicated to serving the living God, Everlasting Father, Creator of all things, and Redeemer or our lives.

The Word says in 1 John 3:2 that one day we shall be like God.[406] As we grow through *student* and *servant*, we will be approaching that as the mission of our lives. Understanding of the truth reveals that he desires to flow into and through us every day in every way. Our calling is to *embrace* that desire and let it happen.

Use understanding of the processes that God has described in this book, supplemented by the "Speak To Share Method" diagram on page 179 as a way to improve your effectiveness in the birth and growth of Christians. During interactions with others, you may sense resistance or lack of growth, which allows you to see they are struggling with a certain *student step*. This awareness can guide you into the most *affective servant role* for their situation. God will not call you to *send* a *student* who is still resistant to *believe*; instead he will call you *speak* and *caress*.

If you have not yet *accepted* Jesus Christ as your Savior and Lord, consider allowing God to treat you as a *student* and cause you to *hear*, then *believe*, then *ask*, then *receive*, then *do*, then *care*, then *show*, and then *share*—all to build a relationship with him and fulfill the first commandment. As your relationship blossoms and matures, he will mature you into a *servant role* and may *teach* you to *speak*, then *caress*, then *offer*, then *bless*, then *teach*, then *mend*, then *empower*, and then *send*. All of these things will be for his glory and our joy, and he will use us to draw others to him. In the *servant role* by God's power and commissioning, we will be walking out the second commandment and fulfilling the Great Commission.[407]

As *servants* of the living God, he will *send* us out to serve him and we will be *operating* in the calling of the Great Commission. His fruit will come within that calling, when we *operate* in the life-style of a God Word for a God reason in a God way and a God time for God's glory.

Discussion Guides

Discussion Guide Overview

Personal growth is often enhanced by repetition and reflection. Each chapter contains a section titled "Reflections and Discussion." That section and the discussion prompts below consist of open-ended questions to promote growth and understanding of material presented in the chapter. Readers are encouraged to consider these discussion questions because they allow individuals to reprocess the chapter, and also promote in-depth group discussions.

Powerful growth can result from consideration of the passages, sections, chapters, and diagrams. Group facilitators are encouraged to focus participants on awareness that God has them learning the material for specific reasons. God wants *students* to get *revelation* about whether or not they are growing, and he wants *servants* to be prepared to understand growth of *students* they may encounter.

Facilitators should choose questions applicable to the group being served, and perhaps offer additional questions not presented here. The following questions generally address first the foundational understanding of the topic and then personal application to foster growth by querying:

1.   What is it?

2.   Why is it important to me?

3.   What are some distractions and interferences?

4.   How does God prepare me for this *step*?

Main Discussion Guide for the Student Process

1.   What does God want to happen in your life during this *step*?

2.   Why is it important in your life to enter this *step*?

3.   What does it mean in your daily life to be maturing in this *step*?

4.   Make a list of the benefits of growing from once or occasionally walking in this *step* to a durative lifestyle of walking in this *step*.

5.   What are some indications that the enemy is trying to prevent growth into and during this *step*? Are any of those indications present in your life?

6.   Make a list of what happens in someone's spiritual walk if they never enter this *step*, staying in the previous *step*.

7.   What kinds of life events or attitudes block someone from *accepting* all that God wants to give them in this *step*? What blockages did you experience?

8.   What did God do in your life to get you ready for this *step*?

9.   Beyond just being made ready, what specific event(s) in your life caused you to release reservations, yield to God's call, and leap into this *step*?

10. What is happening in your heart when you resist *accepting* the growth that God has for you in this *step*?

11. What are your areas of struggle related to this *step*, and what might be preventing you from being victorious in this *step*?

12. Read Matthew 13:1–23. What value is there in being good soil during this *step*? What happens when you are not good soil? What is a good prayer for this situation?

13. What *changed* in your life as you grew during this *step*?

Main Discussion Guide for the Servant Process

1. What does it mean to you to walk out this *role*?

2. What church functions can you think of that *operate* in this *role*?

3. Who do you know that is functioning well in this *role*?

4. List some examples of how God may use a *servant* to pour into a *student* while *operating* in this *role*?

5. How do you know if God has matured you to be ready for this *role*?

6. Why is it important in your life to enter into this *role*?

7. What did God do in your life to get you ready for this *role*?

8. What does God want to happen in your life during this *role*?

9. What evidences are in your life that God is preparing you for this *role*?

10. How do you know if you have been called to this *role*?

11.   How do you see being used in this *role*?

12.   What specific event(s) in your life caused you to allow God to promote you into this *role*?

13.   What does it mean in your daily life to be maturing in this *role*?

14.   What kinds of life events or attitudes block someone from *accepting* all that God wants to give them related to this *role*? What blockages did you experience?

15.   What is happening in your heart when you resist *accepting* the growth that God has for you into this *role*?

16.   What are your areas of struggle related to this *role*, and what might be preventing you from being victorious?

17.   What are some indications that the enemy is trying to prevent growth into and during this *role*? Are any of those indications present in your life?

18.   Make a list of what happens in someone's life if they never enter this *role*, staying in the previous *role*.

19.   What *changed* in your life, as you grew during this *role*?

20.   Make a list of the benefits of growing from occasional to durative/lifestyle *operating* in this *role*.

Appendix

Terms Used throughout the Book

A few terms warrant being presented here to enhance reader understanding.

Period   This represents a time of growth and is the most finite activity noted in the methods. The period describes an action to be completed by either a *student* or a *servant*. One *period of growth* will be completed before the next *period* will be started. Periods are combined together into *seasons* and presented in the chapters titled, "Expanding the Student Process" and "Expanding the Servant Process."

Season   A named collection of periods. *Student Seasons* are preparation, transformation, and celebration. *Servant Seasons* are: preparation, operation, and celebration. The seasons are presented in the chapters titled, "Expanding the Student Process" and "Expanding the Servant Process."

Step   One complete unit of growth of three seasons, with the name of the *step* being used to identify the focus of the growth. A *step* is meant to be completed and used, as a

platform for further growth. In the book, a simplified
view of *step* is initially presented to enhance understanding. This occurs in the first eight chapters of the *student process* and *servant process*. At the end of those two
major portions of the book, the definition of each *step* is
expanded to include the *seasons* noted above. This expansion is detailed in the chapters titled, "Expanding the Student Process" and "Expanding the Servant Process."

Role   Focused longer-term activity in a *step* or in an entire *process*. The *student role* addresses *transformation*, whereas the
servant role addresses *operation* to assist the *student*.

Process   The *student process* is all eight of the *student steps* together.
The *servant process* is all eight of the *servant steps* together.

Method   The "Speak To Share Method:" The *student process* and
the *servant process* together. Salvation occurs on the first
pass through the *student process* while learning the first
commandment. Promotion to *servant* occurs to walk out
the second commandment, and growth is accomplished
in eight *servant steps*. Growth through each *servant step*
involves God sending the *servant* through the *student process* to learn God's way of operating in that role.

Endnotes

Endnotes for Introduction

1 Ephesians 1:17
I keep asking that the God of our Lord Jesus Christ, the glorious Father, may give you the Spirit of wisdom and revelation, so that you may know him better.

2 James 1:17
Every good and perfect gift is from above, coming down from the Father of the heavenly lights, who does not change like shifting shadows.

3 Matthew 10:19–20
But when they arrest you, do not worry about what to say or how to say it. At that time you will be given what to say, for it will not be you speaking, but the Spirit of your Father speaking through you.

4 Proverbs 16:9
In his heart a man plans his course, but the LORD determines his steps.

5 Proverbs 20:24
A man's steps are directed by the LORD …

6   1 Corinthians 3:6
I planted the seed, Apollos watered it, but God made it
grow.

7   Mark 4:13–20
The Parable of the Sower: Then Jesus said to them,
"Don't you understand this parable? How then will you
understand any parable? The farmer sows the word.
Some people are like seed along the path, where the
word is sown. As soon as they hear it, Satan comes and
takes away the word that was sown in them. Others, like
seed sown on rocky places, hear the word and at once
receive it with joy. But since they have no root, they last
only a short time. When trouble or persecution comes
because of the word, they quickly fall away. Still others,
like seed sown among thorns, hear the word; but the
worries of this life, the deceitfulness of wealth and the
desires for other things come in and choke the word,
making it unfruitful. Others, like seed sown on good
soil, hear the word, accept it, and produce a crop—
thirty, sixty or even a hundred times what was sown."

8   Mark 12:29–31
"The most important one," answered Jesus, "is this:
'Hear, O Israel, the Lord our God, the Lord is one. Love
the Lord your God with all your heart and with all your
soul and with all your mind and with all your strength.'
The second is this: 'Love your neighbor as yourself.'
There is no commandment greater than these."

9   Matthew 7:6
"Do not give dogs what is sacred; do not throw your
pearls to pigs. If you do, they may trample them under
their feet, and then turn and tear you to pieces.

Endnotes for Audience

10   1 Corinthians 3:6
I planted the seed, Apollos watered it, but God made it grow.

11   Mark 12:29–31
"The most important one," answered Jesus, "is this: 'Hear, O Israel, the Lord our God, the Lord is one. Love the Lord your God with all your heart and with all your soul and with all your mind and with all your strength.' The second is this: 'Love your neighbor as yourself.' There is no commandment greater than these."

12   Deuteronomy 6:5–7
Love the LORD your God with all your heart and with all your soul and with all your strength. These commandments that I give you today are to be upon your hearts. Impress them on your children. Talk about them when you sit at home and when you walk along the road, when you lie down and when you get up.

Endnotes for Student Process: Learning to Love God

13   Mark 12:29–31
"The most important one," answered Jesus, "is this: 'Hear, O Israel, the Lord our God, the Lord is one. Love the Lord your God with all your heart and with all your soul and with all your mind and with all your strength.' The second is this: 'Love your neighbor as yourself.' There is no commandment greater than these."

14   Deuteronomy 6:5–7
Love the LORD your God with all your heart and with all your soul and with all your strength. These com-

mandments that I give you today are to be upon your hearts. Impress them on your children. Talk about them when you sit at home and when you walk along the road, when you lie down and when you get up.

Endnotes for Hear

15   Luke 10:18
Deception was expelled from heaven: I saw Satan fall like lightning from heaven …

16   Luke 18:16–17
Children can have faith: But Jesus called the children to him and said, "Let the little children come to me, and do not hinder them, for the kingdom of God belongs to such as these. I tell you the truth, anyone who will not receive the kingdom of God like a little child will never enter it."

17   Hebrews 11:1
Now faith is being sure of what we hope for and certain of what we do not see.

18   Matthew 11:15
He who has ears, let him hear.

19   John 3:16
"For God so loved the world that he gave his one and only Son, that whoever believes in him shall not perish but have eternal life.

20   Mark 4:13–20
The Parable of the Sower: Then Jesus said to them, "Don't you understand this parable? How then will you understand any parable? The farmer sows the word. Some people are like seed along the path, where the

word is sown. As soon as they hear it, Satan comes and takes away the word that was sown in them. Others, like seed sown on rocky places, hear the word and at once receive it with joy. But since they have no root, they last only a short time. When trouble or persecution comes because of the word, they quickly fall away. Still others, like seed sown among thorns, hear the word; but the worries of this life, the deceitfulness of wealth and the desires for other things come in and choke the word, making it unfruitful. Others, like seed sown on good soil, hear the word, accept it, and produce a crop— thirty, sixty or even a hundred times what was sown."

21   Matthew 13:19
        When anyone hears the message about the kingdom and does not understand it, the evil one comes and snatches away what was sown in his heart. This is the seed sown along the path.

22   Isaiah 35:5–7
        Then will the eyes of the blind be opened and the ears of the deaf unstopped. Then will the lame leap like a deer, and the mute tongue shout for joy. Water will gush forth in the wilderness and streams in the desert. The burning sand will become a pool, the thirsty ground bubbling springs. In the haunts where jackals once lay, grass and reeds and papyrus will grow.

23   Matthew 18:12
        "What do you think? If a man owns a hundred sheep, and one of them wanders away, will he not leave the ninety-nine on the hills and go to look for the one that wandered off?

24   Luke 5:6
        When they had done so, they caught such a large number of fish that their nets began to break.

25   John 8:47
He who belongs to God hears what God says. The reason you do not hear is that you do not belong to God."

26   Hebrews 3:15
As has just been said: "Today, if you hear his voice, do
not harden your hearts as you did in the rebellion."

27   Romans 10:17
…faith comes from hearing the message, and the message is heard through the word of Christ.

28   1 Corinthians 3:6
I planted the seed, Apollos watered it, but God made it
grow.

29   Luke 11:28
He replied, "Blessed rather are those who hear the word
of God and obey it."

30   Luke 5:5
Simon answered, "Master, we've worked hard all night
and haven't caught anything. But because you say so, I
will let down the nets."

31   1 John 4:1–3
Dear friends, do not believe every spirit, but test the
spirits to see whether they are from God, because many
false prophets have gone out into the world. This is how
you can recognize the Spirit of God: Every spirit that
acknowledges that Jesus Christ has come in the flesh is
from God, but every spirit that does not acknowledge
Jesus is not from God. This is the spirit of the antichrist,
which you have heard is coming and even now is already
in the world.

32   Matthew 11:4-6
      Jesus replied, "Go back and report to John what you
      hear and see: The blind receive sight, the lame walk,
      those who have leprosy are cured, the deaf hear, the dead
      are raised, and the good news is preached to the poor.
      Blessed is the man who does not fall away on account of
      me."

33   Hebrews 4:16
      Let us then approach the throne of grace with confi-
      dence, so that we may receive mercy and find grace to
      help us in our time of need.

34   Jeremiah 13:15
      Hear and pay attention, do not be arrogant, for the
      LORD has spoken.

35   Luke 8:21
      He replied, "My mother and brothers are those who
      hear God's word and put it into practice."

36   Hebrews 6:13–15
      When God made his promise to Abraham, since there
      was no one greater for him to swear by, he swore by him-
      self, saying, "I will surely bless you and give you many
      descendants." And so after waiting patiently, Abraham
      received what was promised.

Endnotes for Believe

37   John 3:16
      "For God so loved the world that he gave his one and
      only Son, that whoever believes in him shall not perish
      but have eternal life.

38   John 20:27
        Then he said to Thomas, "Put your finger here; see my
        hands. Reach out your hand and put it into my side.
        Stop doubting and believe."

39   Genesis 15:6
        Abram believed the Lord, and he credited it to him as
        righteousness.

40   Romans 10:8–10
        But what does it say? "The word is near you; it is in your
        mouth and in your heart," that is, the word of faith we
        are proclaiming: That if you confess with your mouth,
        "Jesus is Lord," and believe in your heart that God
        raised him from the dead, you will be saved. For it is
        with your heart that you believe and are justified, and it
        is with your mouth that you confess and are saved.

41   1 John 4:1
        Test the Spirits: Dear friends, do not believe every
        Spirit, but test the Spirits to see whether they are from
        God, because many false prophets have gone out into
        the world.

42   Acts 2:44
        All the believers were together and had everything in
        common.

43   James 2:19
        You believe that there is one God. Good! Even the
        demons believe that—and shudder.

44   Hebrews 11:1
        Now faith is being sure of what we hope for and certain
        of what we do not see.

45   Luke 10:19
I have given you authority to trample on snakes and scorpions and to overcome all the power of the enemy; nothing will harm you.

46   John 8:44
You belong to your father, the devil, and you want to carry out your father's desire. He was a murderer from the beginning, not holding to the truth, for there is no truth in him. When he lies, he speaks his native language, for he is a liar and the father of lies.

47   Mark 1:25
"Be quiet!" said Jesus sternly. "Come out of him!"

48   1 Corinthians 3:6
I planted the seed, Apollos watered it, but God made it grow.

49   Proverbs 3:5–6
Trust in the LORD with all your heart and lean not on your own understanding; in all your ways acknowledge him, and he will make your paths straight.

50   2 Samuel 11:27–12:1
After the time of mourning was over, David had her brought to his house, and she became his wife and bore him a son. But the thing David had done displeased the LORD. The LORD sent Nathan to David…

51   1 Corinthians 7:16
How do you know, wife, whether you will save your husband? Or, how do you know, husband, whether you will save your wife?

52   Ecclesiastes 3:1–8
There is a time for everything, and a season for every
activity under heaven: a time to be born and a time to
die, a time to plant and a time to uproot, a time to kill
and a time to heal, a time to tear down and a time to
build, a time to weep and a time to laugh, a time to
mourn and a time to dance, a time to scatter stones and
a time to gather them, a time to embrace and a time to
refrain, a time to search and a time to give up, a time to
keep and a time to throw away, a time to tear and a time
to mend, a time to be silent and a time to speak, a time
to love and a time to hate, a time for war and a time for
peace.

53   Acts 16:31
They replied, "Believe in the Lord Jesus, and you will be
saved—you and your household."

54   Matthew 9:27–29
As Jesus went on from there, two blind men followed
him, calling out, "Have mercy on us, Son of David!"
When He had gone indoors, the blind men came to
him, and he asked them, "Do you believe that I am able
to do this?" "Yes, Lord," they replied. Then He touched
their eyes and said, "According to your faith will it be
done to you";

55   Luke 8:43-44
And a woman was there who had been subject to bleeding for twelve years, but no one could heal her. She
came up behind him and touched the edge of his cloak,
and immediately her bleeding stopped.

56   Hebrews 3:15–19
As has just been said: "Today, if you hear his voice, do
not harden your hearts as you did in the rebellion." Who
were they who heard and rebelled? Were they not all

those Moses led out of Egypt? And with whom was he angry for forty years? Was it not with those who sinned, whose bodies fell in the desert? and to whom did God swear that they would never enter his rest if not to those who disobeyed? So we see that they were not able to enter, because of their unbelief.

57   John 8:43–45
Why is my language not clear to you? Because you are unable to hear what I say. You belong to your father, the devil, and you want to carry out your father's desire. He was a murderer from the beginning, not holding to the truth, for there is no truth in him. When he lies, he speaks his native language, for he is a liar and the father of lies. Yet because I tell the truth, you do not believe me!

58   Mark 3:5–6
He looked around at them in anger and, deeply distressed at their stubborn hearts, said to the man, "Stretch out your hand." He stretched it out, and his hand was completely restored. Then the Pharisees went out and began to plot with the Herodians how they might kill Jesus.

59   Luke 11:7–10
"Then the one inside answers, 'Don't bother me. The door is already locked, and my children are with me in bed. I can't get up and give you anything.' I tell you, though he will not get up and give him the bread because he is his friend, yet because of the man's boldness he will get up and give him as much as he needs. "So I say to you: Ask and it will be given to you; seek and you will find; knock and the door will be opened to you. For everyone who asks receives; he who seeks finds; and to him who knocks, the door will be opened.

60   Mark 9:23–24
"'If you can'?" said Jesus. "Everything is possible for him who believes." Immediately the boy's father exclaimed, "I do believe; help me overcome my unbelief!"

61   Luke 15:20
So he got up and went to his father. "But while he was still a long way off, his father saw him and was filled with compassion for him; he ran to his son, threw his arms around him and kissed him.

62   Isaiah 61:11
For as the soil makes the sprout come up and a garden causes seeds to grow, so the Sovereign LORD will make righteousness (believing God) and praise spring up before all nations.

63   Psalm 127:1
Unless the LORD builds the house, its builders labor in vain. Unless the LORD watches over the city, the watchmen stand guard in vain.

64   Acts 9:3
As he neared Damascus on his journey, suddenly a light from heaven flashed around him.

65   Romans 10:10
For it is with your heart that you believe and are justified, and it is with your mouth that you confess and are saved.

66   John 8:32
Then you will know the truth, and the truth will set you free."

67   Isaiah 43:10
         "You are my witnesses," declares the Lord, "and my ser-
         vant whom I have chosen, so that you may know and
         believe me and understand that I am he…"

68   Galatians 3:5
         Does God give you his Spirit and work miracles among
         you because you observe the law, or because you believe
         what you heard?

Endnotes for Ask

69   Matthew 21:22
         Believe–Ask–Receive: "If you believe, you will receive
         whatever you ask for in prayer."

70   Matthew 18:19
         "Again, I tell you that if two of you on earth agree about
         anything you ask for, it will be done for you by my
         Father in heaven.

71   Luke 11:9–10
         "So I say to you: ask and it will be given to you; seek and
         you will find; knock and the door will be opened to you.
         For everyone who asks receives; he who seeks finds; and
         to him who knocks, the door will be opened.

72   Matthew 7:7
         "Ask and it will be given to you; seek and you will find;
         knock and the door will be opened to you.

73   John 14:13–14
         And I will do whatever you ask in my name, so that the
         Son may bring glory to the Father. You may ask me for
         anything in my name, and I will do it.

74   Mark 11:24
Believe–Ask–Receive: Therefore I tell you, whatever
you ask for in prayer, believe that you have received it,
and it will be yours.

75   Matthew 28:18
Then Jesus came to them and said, "All authority in
heaven and on earth has been given to me.

76   1 Corinthians 1:18
For the message of the cross is foolishness to those who
are perishing, but to us who are being saved it is the
power of God.

77   Jeremiah 29:13
You will seek me and find me when you seek me with all
your heart.

78   James 1:17
Every good and perfect gift is from above, coming
down from the Father of the heavenly lights, who does
not change like shifting shadows.

79   Proverbs 14:12
There is a way that seems right to a man, but in the end
it leads to death.

80   Hebrews 6:18
God cannot lie: God did this so that, by two unchangeable things in which it is impossible for God to lie, we
who have fled to take hold of the hope offered to us may
be greatly encouraged.

81   James 4:3
When you ask, you do not receive, because you ask with
wrong motives, that you may spend what you get on
your pleasures.

82   Psalm 23:5
        You prepare a table before me in the presence of my
        enemies. You anoint my head with oil; my cup overflows.

83   1 Corinthians 3:6
        I planted the seed, Apollos watered it, but God made it
        grow.

84   Hebrews 4:16
        Let us then approach the throne of grace with confidence, so that we may receive mercy and find grace to
        help us in our time of need.

85   John 16:23–24
        In that day you will no longer ask me anything. I tell
        you the truth, my Father will give you whatever you ask
        in my name. Until now you have not asked for anything
        in my name. Ask and you will receive, and your joy will
        be complete.

86   James 4:2
        You want something but don't get it. You kill and covet,
        but you cannot have what you want. You quarrel and
        fight. You do not have, because you do not ask God.

87   John 5:24
        "I tell you the truth, whoever hears my word and
        believes him who sent me has eternal life and will not
        be condemned; he has crossed over from death to life.

88   James 1:5–6
        Asking for Wisdom: If any of you lacks wisdom, he
        should ask God, who gives generously to all without
        finding fault, and it will be given to him. But when he
        asks, he must believe and not doubt …

Endnotes for Receive

89   1 Thessalonians 5:9
        (God appointed us)…to receive salvation through our
        Lord Jesus Christ.

90   John 1:12
        Yet to all who received him, to those who believed in his
        name, he gave the right to become children of God—

91   Matthew 16:17
        Jesus replied, "Blessed are you, Simon son of Jonah, for
        this was not revealed to you by man, but by my Father
        in heaven.

92   Colossians 2:6
        So then, just as you received Christ Jesus as Lord, con-
        tinue to live in him,

93   Acts 19:2
        and asked them, "Did you receive the Holy Spirit when
        you believed?" They answered, "No, we have not even
        heard that there is a Holy Spirit."

94   Acts 19:6
        When Paul placed his hands on them, the Holy
        Spirit came on them, and they spoke in tongues and
        prophesied.

95   Luke 18:29–30
        "I tell you the truth," Jesus said to them, "no one who
        has left home or wife or brothers or parents or children
        for the sake of the kingdom of God will fail to receive
        many times as much in this age and, in the age to come,
        eternal life."

96   John 8:32
          Then you will know the truth, and the truth will set you
          free.”

97   Matthew 25:21
          “His master replied, ‘Well done, good and faithful ser-
          vant! You have been faithful with a few things; I will
          put you in charge of many things. Come and share your
          master’s happiness!’

98   John 3:27
          To this John replied, “A man can receive only what is
          given him from heaven.

99   Romans 8:15
          …but you received the Spirit of sonship…

100   Galatians 3:14
          …by faith we might receive the promise of the Spirit.

101   Matthew 13:20–23
          Parable of the Sower: The one who received the seed
          that fell on rocky places is the man who hears the word
          and at once receives it with joy. But since he has no root,
          he lasts only a short time. When trouble or persecution
          comes because of the word, he quickly falls away. The
          one who received the seed that fell among the thorns
          is the man who hears the word, but the worries of this
          life and the deceitfulness of wealth choke it, making it
          unfruitful. But the one who received the seed that fell
          on good soil is the man who hears the word and under-
          stands it. He produces a crop, yielding a hundred, sixty
          or thirty times what was sown.”

102   Luke 18:42–43
          Jesus offers and the blind man accepts: Jesus said to
          him, “Receive your sight; your faith has healed you.”

Immediately he received his sight and followed Jesus, praising God. When all the people saw it, they also praised God.

103   Mark 10:52
"Go," said Jesus, "your faith has healed you." Immediately he received his sight and followed Jesus along the road.

104   Luke 18:17
I tell you the truth, anyone who will not receive the kingdom of God like a little child will never enter it."

105   Acts 10:46
For they heard them speaking in tongues and praising God.

106   Psalm 23:4
Even though I walk through the valley of the shadow of death, I will fear no evil, for you are with me; your rod and your staff, they comfort me.

107   Proverbs 3:11–12
My son, do not despise the LORD's discipline and do not resent his rebuke, because the LORD disciplines those he loves, as a father the son he delights in.

108   James 4:3
Nothing is offered: When you ask, you do not receive, because you ask with wrong motives, that you may spend what you get on your pleasures.

109   1 Corinthians 2:14
The man without the Spirit does not accept the things that come from the Spirit of God…

110   James 1:6–8
        But when he asks, he must believe and not doubt,
        because he who doubts is like a wave of the sea, blown
        and tossed by the wind. That man should not think he
        will receive anything (offered) from the Lord; he is a
        double-minded man, unstable in all he does.

111   John 10:10
        The thief comes only to steal and kill and destroy; I
        have come that they may have life, and have it to the
        full.

112   John 8:44
        You belong to your father, the devil, and you want to
        carry out your father's desire. He was a murderer from
        the beginning, not holding to the truth, for there is no
        truth in him. When he lies, he speaks his native lan-
        guage, for he is a liar and the father of lies.

113   1 Corinthians 3:6
        I planted the seed, Apollos watered it, but God made it
        grow.

114   Deuteronomy 30:16
        For I command you today to love the LORD your God,
        to walk in his ways, and to keep his commands, decrees
        and laws; then you will live and increase, and the LORD
        your God will bless you in the land you are entering to
        possess.

115   Isaiah 52:1–3
        Awake, awake, O Zion, clothe yourself with strength.
        Put on your garments of splendor, O Jerusalem, the
        holy city. The uncircumcised and defiled will not enter
        you again. Shake off your dust; rise up, sit enthroned, O
        Jerusalem. Free yourself from the chains on your neck,
        O captive Daughter of Zion. For this is what the LORD

says: "You were sold for nothing, and without money you will be redeemed."

116   Romans 2:4
Or do you show contempt for the riches of his kindness, tolerance and patience, not realizing that God's kindness leads you toward repentance?

117   Isaiah 55:8–11
"For my thoughts are not your thoughts, neither are your ways my ways," declares the Lord. "As the heavens are higher than the earth, so are my ways higher than your ways and my thoughts than your thoughts. As the rain and the snow come down from heaven, and do not return to it without watering the earth and making it bud and flourish, so that it yields seed for the Sower and bread for the eater, so is my word that goes out from my mouth: It will not return to me empty, but will accomplish what I desire and achieve the purpose for which I sent it.

118   1 John 1:7
But if we walk in the light, as he is in the light, we have fellowship with one another, and the blood of Jesus, his Son, purifies us from all sin.

119   Ephesians 1:7
In him we have redemption through his blood, the forgiveness of sins, in accordance with the riches of God's grace

120   2 Peter 1:11
and you will receive a rich welcome into the eternal kingdom of our Lord and Savior Jesus Christ.

121   John 3:16
"For God so loved the world that he gave his one and only Son, that whoever believes in him shall not perish but have eternal life.

122   1 Peter 1:23
For you have been born again, not of perishable seed, but of imperishable, through the living and enduring word of God.

123   Matthew 7:21
"Not everyone who says to me, 'Lord, Lord,' will enter the kingdom of heaven, but only he who does the will of my Father who is in heaven.

124   Job 38:1–4
Then the LORD answered Job out of the storm. He said: "Who is this that darkens my counsel with words without knowledge? Brace yourself like a man; I will question you, and you shall answer me. "Where were you when I laid the earth's foundation? Tell me, if you understand.

Endnotes for Do

125   James 1:22, 25
Do the word of God (Be a doer and not just a hearer only): do not merely listen to the word, and so deceive yourselves. Do what it says … But the man who looks intently into the perfect law that gives freedom, and continues to do this, not forgetting what he has heard, but doing it—he will be blessed in what he does.

126   Luke 11:28
Doing God's Word will cause you to be blessed: He replied, "Blessed rather are those who hear the word of God and obey it."

127   Luke 6:46
           "Why do you call me, 'Lord, Lord,' and do not do what
           I say?

128   Romans 3:28
           For we maintain that a man is justified by faith apart
           from observing the law.

129   Jeremiah 17:9
           The heart is deceitful above all things and beyond cure.
           Who can understand it?

130   Acts 3:6
           Then Peter said, "Silver or gold I do not have, but what
           I have I give you. In the name of Jesus Christ of Naza-
           reth, walk."

131   Luke 10:9
           Heal the sick who are there and tell them, 'The king-
           dom of God is near you.'

132   James 5:15
           And the prayer offered in faith will make the sick per-
           son well; the Lord will raise him up. If he has sinned, he
           will be forgiven.

133   Romans 12:2
           Do not conform any longer to the pattern of this world,
           but be transformed by the renewing of your mind. Then
           you will be able to test and approve what God's will
           is—his good, pleasing and perfect will.

134   Matthew 8:5–13
           When Jesus had entered Capernaum, a centurion came
           to him, asking for help. "Lord," he said, "my servant lies
           at home paralyzed and in terrible suffering." Jesus said
           to him, "I will go and heal him." The centurion replied,

"Lord, I do not deserve to have you come under my roof. But just say the word, and my servant will be healed. For I myself am a man under authority, with soldiers under me. I tell this one, 'Go,' and he goes; and that one, 'Come,' and he comes. I say to my servant, 'Do this,' and he does it." When Jesus heard this, he was astonished and said to those following him, "I tell you the truth, I have not found anyone in Israel with such great faith. I say to you that many will come from the east and the west, and will take their places at the feast with Abraham, Isaac and Jacob in the kingdom of heaven. But the subjects of the kingdom will be thrown outside, into the darkness, where there will be weeping and gnashing of teeth." Then Jesus said to the centurion, "Go! It will be done just as you believed it would." And his servant was healed at that very hour.

135   1 Corinthians 2:15
The spiritual man makes judgments about all things, but he himself is not subject to any man's judgment:

136   Matthew 7:15–20
"Watch out for false prophets. They come to you in sheep's clothing, but inwardly they are ferocious wolves. By their fruit you will recognize them. Do people pick grapes from thornbushes, or figs from thistles? Likewise every good tree bears good fruit, but a bad tree bears bad fruit. A good tree cannot bear bad fruit, and a bad tree cannot bear good fruit. Every tree that does not bear good fruit is cut down and thrown into the fire. Thus, by their fruit you will recognize them.

137   Matthew 16:11–12
How is it you don't understand that I was not talking to you about bread? But be on your guard against the yeast of the Pharisees and Sadducees." Then they understood that he was not telling them to guard against the yeast

used in bread, but against the teaching of the Pharisees and Sadducees.

138   Proverbs 27:17
        As iron sharpens iron, so one man sharpens another.

139   Genesis 4:4-8
        …The Lord looked with favor on Abel and his offering, but on Cain and his offering he did not look with favor. So Cain was very angry, and his face was downcast. Then the Lord said to Cain, "Why are you angry? Why is your face downcast? If you do what is right, will you not be accepted? But if you do not do what is right, sin is crouching at your door; it desires to have you, but you must master it." Now Cain said to his brother Abel, "Let's go out to the field." And while they were in the field, Cain attacked his brother Abel and killed him.

140   Proverbs 14:12
        There is a way that seems right to a man, but in the end it leads to death.

141   Romans 2:4
        Or do you show contempt for the riches of his kindness, tolerance and patience, not realizing that God's kindness leads you toward repentance?

142   Matthew 16:17
        Jesus replied, "Blessed are you, Simon son of Jonah, for this was not revealed to you by man, but by my Father in heaven."

143   John 8:31–32
        To the Jews who had believed him, Jesus said, "If you hold to my teaching, you are really my disciples. Then you will know the truth, and the truth will set you free."

144   Romans 2:13
          For it is not those who hear the law who are righteous
          in God's sight, but it is those who obey the law who will
          be declared righteous.

145   Mark 12:29–31
          "The most important one," answered Jesus, "is this:
          'Hear, O Israel, the Lord our God, the Lord is one. Love
          the Lord your God with all your heart and with all your
          soul and with all your mind and with all your strength.'
          The second is this: 'Love your neighbor as yourself.'
          There is no commandment greater than these."

146   Colossians 3:13
          Bear with each other and forgive whatever grievances
          you may have against one another. Forgive as the Lord
          forgave you.

147   Galatians 5:1
          It is for freedom that Christ has set us free. Stand firm,
          then, and do not let yourselves be burdened again by a
          yoke of slavery.

148   Revelation 12:11
          They overcame him by the blood of the Lamb and by
          the word of their testimony; they did not love their lives
          so much as to shrink from death.

149   Matthew 7:21,24
          "Not everyone who says to me, 'Lord, Lord,' will enter
          the kingdom of heaven, but only he who does the will
          of my Father who is in heaven…"Therefore every-
          one who hears these words of mine and puts (words of
          Jesus) them into practice is like a wise man who built
          his house on the rock.

150   John 8:31–32
To the Jews who had believed him, Jesus said, "If you hold to my teaching, you are really my disciples. Then you will know the truth, and the truth will set you free."

151   Isaiah 55:8–11
"For my thoughts are not your thoughts, neither are your ways my ways," declares the LORD. "As the heavens are higher than the earth, so are my ways higher than your ways and my thoughts than your thoughts. As the rain and the snow come down from heaven, and do not return to it without watering the earth and making it bud and flourish, so that it yields seed for the Sower and bread for the eater, so is my word that goes out from my mouth: It will not return to me empty, but will accomplish what I desire and achieve the purpose for which I sent it.

152   Acts 2:38
Peter replied, "Repent and be baptized, every one of you, in the name of Jesus Christ for the forgiveness of your sins. And you will receive the gift of the Holy Spirit.

153   Acts 3:26
When God raised up his servant, he sent him first to you to bless you by turning each of you from your wicked ways."

Endnotes for Care

154   Romans 12:2
Do not conform any longer to the pattern of this world, but be transformed by the renewing of your mind…

155   2 Timothy 1:14
Guard the good deposit that was entrusted to you—guard it with the help of the Holy Spirit who lives in us.

156   2 Timothy 1:6
          For this reason I remind you to fan into flame the gift
          of God, which is in you through the laying on of my
          hands.

157   Matthew 12:22
          Then they brought him a demon-possessed man who
          was blind and mute, and Jesus healed him, so that he
          could both talk and see.

158   Matthew 13:44
          The kingdom of heaven is like treasure hidden in a field.
          When a man found it, he hid it again, and then in his
          joy went and sold all he had and bought that field.

159   2 Timothy 1:14
          Guard the good deposit that was entrusted to you—
          guard it with the help of the Holy Spirit who lives in us.

160   1 Timothy 6:20
          Timothy, guard what has been entrusted to your care.
          Turn away from Godless chatter and the opposing ideas
          of what is falsely called knowledge,

161   Joshua 1:7
          Caretake the Truth: Be strong and very courageous. Be
          careful to obey all the law my servant Moses gave you;
          do not turn from it to the right or to the left, that you
          may be successful wherever you go.

162   Proverbs 7:2
          Keep my commands and you will live; guard my teach-
          ings as the apple of your eye.

163   Proverbs 4:13
          Care for instructions given to you: Hold on to instruc-
          tion, do not let it go; guard it well, for it is your life.

164   Genesis 2:15
The Lord God took the man and put him in the Garden of Eden to work it and take care of it.

165   Mark 4:13–20
The Parable of the Sower: Then Jesus said to them, "Don't you understand this parable? How then will you understand any parable? The farmer sows the word. Some people are like seed along the path, where the word is sown. As soon as they hear it, Satan comes and takes away the word that was sown in them. Others, like seed sown on rocky places, hear the word and at once receive it with joy. But since they have no root, they last only a short time. When trouble or persecution comes because of the word, they quickly fall away. Still others, like seed sown among thorns, hear the word; but the worries of this life, the deceitfulness of wealth and the desires for other things come in and choke the word, making it unfruitful. Others, like seed sown on good soil, hear the word, accept it, and produce a crop—thirty, sixty or even a hundred times what was sown."

166   Philippians 2:12–13
Therefore, my dear friends, as you have always obeyed—not only in my presence, but now much more in my absence—continue to work out your salvation with fear and trembling, for it is God who works in you to will and to act according to his good purpose.

167   1 Corinthians 3:6
I planted the seed, Apollos watered it, but God made it grow.

168   Romans 9:21
Does not the potter have the right to make out of the same lump of clay some pottery for noble purposes and some for common use?

169   John 10:10
           The thief comes only to steal and kill and destroy; I
           have come that they may have life, and have it to the
           full.

170   2 Peter 3:17
           Therefore, dear friends, since you already know this,
           be on your guard so that you may not be carried away
           by the error of lawless men and fall from your secure
           position.

171   Matthew 6:1
           "Be careful not to do your 'acts of righteousness' before
           men, to be seen by them. If you do, you will have no
           reward from your Father in heaven.

172   Deuteronomy 20:18
           Otherwise, they will teach you to follow all the detest-
           able things they do in worshiping their gods, and you
           will sin against the LORD your God.

173   Matthew 13:44
           "The kingdom of heaven is like treasure hidden in a
           field. When a man found it, he hid it again, and then in
           his joy went and sold all he had and bought that field.

174   John 8:44
           You belong to your father, the devil, and you want to
           carry out your father's desire. He was a murderer from
           the beginning, not holding to the truth, for there is no
           truth in him. When he lies, he speaks his native lan-
           guage, for he is a liar and the father of lies.

175   Philippians 4:8
           Finally, brothers, whatever is true, whatever is noble,
           whatever is right, whatever is pure, whatever is lovely,
           whatever is admirable—if anything is excellent or
           praiseworthy—think about such things.

176   Philippians 4:13
           I can do everything through him who gives me strength.

177   Isaiah 55:11
           so is my word that goes out from my mouth: It will not
           return to me empty, but will accomplish what I desire
           and achieve the purpose for which I sent it.

178   James 1:22
           Do not merely listen to the word, and so deceive your-
           selves. Do what it says.

179   Isaiah 55:8–11
           "For my thoughts are not your thoughts, neither are
           your ways my ways," declares the LORD. "As the heavens
           are higher than the earth, so are my ways higher than
           your ways and my thoughts than your thoughts. As the
           rain and the snow come down from heaven, and do not
           return to it without watering the earth and making it
           bud and flourish, so that it yields seed for the Sower and
           bread for the eater, so is my word that goes out from my
           mouth: It will not return to me empty, but will accom-
           plish what I desire and achieve the purpose for which I
           sent it.

180   James 1:17
           Every good and perfect gift is from above, coming
           down from the Father of the heavenly lights, who does
           not change like shifting shadows.

181   Romans 3:23
           for all have sinned and fall short of the glory of God,

182   Hebrews 13:8
           Jesus Christ is the same yesterday and today and forever.

183   Romans 12:2
          Do not conform any longer to the pattern of this world,
          but be transformed by the renewing of your mind. Then
          you will be able to test and approve what God's will
          is—his good, pleasing and perfect will.

184   1 Corinthians 2:9
          However, as it is written: "No eye has seen, no ear has
          heard, no mind has conceived what God has prepared
          for those who love him"—

185   2 Corinthians 10:17
          But, "Let him who boasts boast in the Lord."

186   Hebrews 6:15
          And so after waiting patiently, Abraham received what
          was promised.

Endnotes for Show

187   Galatians 5:22–23
          But the fruit of the Spirit is love, joy, peace, patience,
          kindness, goodness, faithfulness, gentleness and
          self-control…

188   2 Timothy 2:15
          Show yourself to God: Do your best to present yourself
          to God as one approved, a workman who does not need
          to be ashamed and who correctly handles the word of
          truth.

189   James 2:18
          But someone will say, "You have faith; I have deeds."
          Show me your faith without deeds, and I will show you
          my faith by what I do.

190 1 Peter 2:12
Live such good lives among the pagans that, though they accuse you of doing wrong, they may see your good deeds and glorify God on the day he visits us.

191 Titus 2:7–8
In everything set them an example by doing what is good. In your teaching show integrity, seriousness and soundness of speech that cannot be condemned, so that those who oppose you may be ashamed because they have nothing bad to say about us.

192 Psalm 37:6
God shows us off: He will make your righteousness shine like the dawn, the justice of your cause like the noonday sun.

193 James 4:6
But he gives us more grace. That is why Scripture says: "God opposes the proud but gives grace to the humble."

194 2 Corinthians 3:18
And we, who with unveiled faces all reflect the Lord's glory, are being transformed into his likeness with ever-increasing glory, which comes from the Lord, who is the Spirit.

195 Ephesians 4:22–24
You were taught, with regard to your former way of life, to put off your old self, which is being corrupted by its deceitful desires; to be made new in the attitude of your minds; and to put on the new self, created to be like God in true righteousness and holiness.

196 Titus 3:2
… show true humility toward all men.

197   James 3:17
        But the wisdom that comes from heaven is first of all
        pure; then peace—loving, considerate, submissive, full
        of mercy and good fruit, impartial and sincere.

198   Romans 2:4
        Or do you show contempt for the riches of his kindness,
        tolerance and patience, not realizing that God's kind-
        ness leads you toward repentance?

199   Matthew 12:16
        warning them not to tell who he was.

200   Matthew 5:16
        In the same way, let your light shine before men, that
        they may see your good deeds and praise your Father in
        heaven.

201   Acts 10:34
        Then Peter began to speak: "I now realize how true it is
        that God does not show favoritism

202   Matthew 25:21
        "His master replied, 'Well done, good and faithful ser-
        vant! You have been faithful with a few things; I will
        put you in charge of many things. Come and share your
        master's happiness!'

203   Mark 4:13–20
        The Parable of the Sower: Then Jesus said to them,
        "Don't you understand this parable? How then will you
        understand any parable? The farmer sows the word.
        Some people are like seed along the path, where the
        word is sown. As soon as they hear it, Satan comes and
        takes away the word that was sown in them. Others, like
        seed sown on rocky places, hear the word and at once
        receive it with joy. But since they have no root, they last

only a short time. When trouble or persecution comes because of the word, they quickly fall away. Still others, like seed sown among thorns, hear the word; but the worries of this life, the deceitfulness of wealth and the desires for other things come in and choke the word, making it unfruitful. Others, like seed sown on good soil, hear the word, accept it, and produce a crop—thirty, sixty or even a hundred times what was sown."

204   Deuteronomy 30:19
This day I call heaven and earth as witnesses against you that I have set before you life and death, blessings and curses. Now choose life, so that you and your children may live

205   Revelation 4:10–11
the twenty-four elders fall down before him who sits on the throne, and worship him who lives for ever and ever. They lay their crowns before the throne and say: "You are worthy, our Lord and God, to receive glory and honor and power, for you created all things, and by your will they were created and have their being."

206   Philippians 4:8
Finally, brothers, whatever is true, whatever is noble, whatever is right, whatever is pure, whatever is lovely, whatever is admirable—if anything is excellent or praiseworthy—think about such things.

207   Matthew 6:5–6
"And when you pray, do not be like the hypocrites, for they love to pray standing in the synagogues and on the street corners to be seen by men. I tell you the truth, they have received their reward in full. But when you pray, go into your room, close the door and pray to your Father, who is unseen. Then your Father, who sees what is done in secret, will reward you.

Endnotes for Share

208   Isaiah 6:8–9
Then I heard the voice of the Lord saying, "Whom shall I send? And who will go for us?" And I said, "Here am I. Send me!" He said, "Go and tell this people: " 'Be ever hearing, but never understanding; be ever seeing, but never perceiving.'

209   Hebrews 13:20–21
God equips for doing his will: May the God of peace, who through the blood of the eternal covenant brought back from the dead our Lord Jesus, that great Shepherd of the sheep, equip you with everything good for doing his will, and may he work in us what is pleasing to him, through Jesus Christ, to whom be glory for ever and ever. Amen.

210   Matthew 4:10
Jesus said to him, "Away from me, Satan! For it is written: 'Worship the Lord your God, and serve him only.' "

211   Luke 22:26
But you are not to be like that. Instead, the greatest among you should be like the youngest, and the one who rules like the one who serves.

212   Matthew 10:8
Freely share the gifts of God for the body: "Heal the sick, raise the dead, cleanse those who have leprosy, drive out demons. Freely you have received, freely give.

213   1 Corinthians 12:28
And in the church God has appointed first of all apostles, second prophets, third teachers, then workers of miracles, also those having gifts of healing, those able

to help others, those with gifts of administration, and those speaking in different kinds of tongues.

214   Romans 1:1
Paul, a servant of Christ Jesus, called to be an apostle and set apart for the gospel of God—

215   John 10:38
But if I do it, even though you do not believe me, believe the miracles, that you may know and understand that the Father is in me, and I in the Father."

216   Acts 2:40–41
With many other words he warned them; and he pleaded with them, "Save yourselves from this corrupt generation." Those who accepted his message were baptized, and about three thousand were added to their number that day.

217   Exodus 4:11–15
The Lord said to him, "Who gave man his mouth? Who makes him deaf or mute? Who gives him sight or makes him blind? Is it not I, the Lord? Now go; I will help you speak and will teach you what to say." But Moses said, "O Lord, please send someone else to do it." Then the Lord's anger burned against Moses and he said, "What about your brother, Aaron the Levite? I know he can speak well. He is already on his way to meet you, and his heart will be glad when he sees you. You shall speak to him and put words in his mouth; I will help both of you speak and will teach you what to do.

218   Judges 6:15,36–40
"But Lord," Gideon asked, "how can I save Israel? My clan is the weakest in Manasseh, and I am the least in my family." … Gideon said to God, "If you will save

Israel by my hand as you have promised— look, I will place a wool fleece on the threshing floor. If there is dew only on the fleece and all the ground is dry, then I will know that you will save Israel by my hand, as you said." And that is what happened. Gideon rose early the next day; he squeezed the fleece and wrung out the dew—a bowlful of water. Then Gideon said to God, "Do not be angry with me. Let me make just one more request. Allow me one more test with the fleece. This time make the fleece dry and the ground covered with dew." That night God did so. Only the fleece was dry; all the ground was covered with dew.

219   1 Corinthians 3:6
        I planted the seed, Apollos watered it, but God made it grow.

220   Psalm 127:1
        Unless the LORD builds the house, its builders labor in vain. Unless the LORD watches over the city, the watchmen stand guard in vain.

221   Philippians 4:13
        I can do everything through him who gives me strength.

222   Matthew 22:37–40
        Jesus replied: " 'Love the Lord your God with all your heart and with all your soul and with all your mind.' This is the first and greatest commandment. And the second is like it: 'Love your neighbor as yourself.' All the Law and the Prophets hang on these two commandments."

223   Matthew 28:18–20
        Then Jesus came to them and said, "All authority in heaven and on earth has been given to me. Therefore go and make disciples of all nations, baptizing them in the name of the Father and of the Son and of the Holy

Spirit, and teaching them to obey everything I have commanded you. And surely I am with you always, to the very end of the age."

224   1 Corinthians 1:27
        But God chose the foolish things of the world to shame the wise; God chose the weak things of the world to shame the strong.

225   John 9:15
        Therefore the Pharisees also asked him how he had received his sight. "He put mud on my eyes," the man replied, "and I washed, and now I see."

226   John 9:25
        He replied, "Whether he is a sinner or not, I don't know. One thing I do know. I was blind but now I see!"

227   Revelation 12:11
        They overcame him by the blood of the Lamb and by the word of their testimony; they did not love their lives so much as to shrink from death.

228   Acts 16:31
        They replied, "Believe in the Lord Jesus, and you will be saved—you and your household."

229   John 4:53
        Then the father realized that this was the exact time at which Jesus had said to him, "Your son will live." So he and all his household believed.

230   Luke 12:11–12
        "When you are brought before synagogues, rulers and authorities, do not worry about how you will defend yourselves or what you will say, for the Holy Spirit will teach you at that time what you should say."

231   Mark 13:11
           Whenever you are arrested and brought to trial, do not
           worry beforehand about what to say. Just say whatever
           is given you at the time, for it is not you speaking, but
           the Holy Spirit.

Endnotes for Expanding the Student Process

232   Joshua 13:1
           When Joshua was old and well advanced in years, the
           Lord said to him, "You are very old, and there are still
           very large areas of land to be taken over.

Endnotes for Servant Role: Giving God Away

233   Mark 12:29–31
           "The most important one," answered Jesus, "is this:
           'Hear, O Israel, the Lord our God, the Lord is one. Love
           the Lord your God with all your heart and with all your
           soul and with all your mind and with all your strength.'
           The second is this: 'Love your neighbor as yourself.'
           There is no commandment greater than these."

234   Mark 16:15–16
           He said to them, "Go into all the world and preach the
           good news to all creation. Whoever believes and is bap-
           tized will be saved, but whoever does not believe will be
           condemned.

235   Mark 16:16
           Whoever believes and is baptized will be saved, but
           whoever does not believe will be condemned.

236   Romans 3:23
           for all have sinned and fall short of the glory of God,

237   Romans 12:2
            Do not conform any longer to the pattern of this world,
            but be transformed by the renewing of your mind. Then
            you will be able to test and approve what God's will
            is—his good, pleasing and perfect will.

238   Psalm 127:1
            Unless the LORD builds the house, its builders labor in
            vain. Unless the LORD watches over the city, the watch-
            men stand guard in vain.

239   Matthew 18:21–22
            Then Peter came to Jesus and asked, "Lord, how many
            times shall I forgive my brother when he sins against
            me? Up to seven times?" Jesus answered, "I tell you, not
            seven times, but seventy-seven times.

240   Philippians 3:12
            Not that I have already obtained all this, or have already
            been made perfect, but I press on to take hold of that for
            which Christ Jesus took hold of me.

241   Matthew 9:37–38
            Then he said to his disciples, "The harvest is plentiful
            but the workers are few. Ask the Lord of the harvest,
            therefore, to send out workers into his harvest field."

242   Luke 15:4
            "Suppose one of you has a hundred sheep and loses one
            of them. Does he not leave the ninety-nine in the open
            country and go after the lost sheep until he finds it?

243   John 21:17
The third time he said to him, "Simon son of John, do you love me?" Peter was hurt because Jesus asked him the third time, "Do you love me?" He said, "Lord, you know all things; you know that I love you." Jesus said, "Feed my sheep.

244   Matthew 20:26
Not so with you. Instead, whoever wants to become great among you must be your servant,

245   Colossians 1:25
I have become its servant by the commission God gave me to present to you the word of God in its fullness—

246   Isaiah 35:5–7
Then will the eyes of the blind be opened and the ears of the deaf unstopped. Then will the lame leap like a deer, and the mute tongue shout for joy. Water will gush forth in the wilderness and streams in the desert. The burning sand will become a pool, the thirsty ground bubbling springs. In the haunts where jackals once lay, grass and reeds and papyrus will grow.

Endnotes for Speak

247   Isaiah 55:11
so is my word that goes out from my mouth: It will not return to me empty, but will accomplish what I desire and achieve the purpose for which I sent it.

248   Hebrews 6:18
God did this so that, by two unchangeable things in which it is impossible for God to lie, we who have fled to take hold of the hope offered to us may be greatly encouraged.

249   Romans 10:17
           …faith comes from hearing the message, and the mes-
           sage is heard through the word of Christ.

250   Matthew 16:17
           Jesus replied, "Blessed are you, Simon son of Jonah, for
           this was not revealed to you by man, but by my Father
           in heaven.

251   John 5:19
           Jesus gave them this answer: "I tell you the truth, the
           Son can do nothing by himself; he can do only what he
           sees his Father doing, because whatever the Father does
           the Son also does.

252   Ephesians 5:19
           Speak to one another with psalms, hymns and spiritual
           songs. Sing and make music in your heart to the Lord,

253   Isaiah 35:4
           say to those with fearful hearts, "Be strong, do not fear;
           your God will come, he will come with vengeance; with
           divine retribution he will come to save you."

254   2 Timothy 3:17
           so that the man of God may be thoroughly equipped for
           every good work.

255   James 4:7
           Submit yourselves, then, to God. Resist the devil, and
           he will flee from you.

256   John 8:44
           You belong to your father, the devil, and you want to
           carry out your father's desire. He was a murderer from
           the beginning, not holding to the truth, for there is no
           truth in him. When he lies, he speaks his native lan-
           guage, for he is a liar and the father of lies.

257   Romans 10:14–15
How, then, can they call on the one they have not believed in? And how can they believe in the one of whom they have not heard? And how can they hear without someone preaching to them? And how can they preach unless they are sent? As it is written, "How beautiful are the feet of those who bring good news!"

258   Psalm 127:1
Unless the LORD builds the house, its builders labor in vain. Unless the LORD watches over the city, the watchmen stand guard in vain.

259   2 Peter 1:21
…but (prophetic) men spoke from God as they were carried along by the Holy Spirit.

260   1 John 1:7
But if we walk in the light, as he is in the light, we have fellowship with one another, and the blood of Jesus, his Son, purifies us from all sin.

261   Mark 4:13–20
The Parable of the Sower: Then Jesus said to them, "Don't you understand this parable? How then will you understand any parable? The farmer sows the word. Some people are like seed along the path, where the word is sown. As soon as they hear it, Satan comes and takes away the word that was sown in them. Others, like seed sown on rocky places, hear the word and at once receive it with joy. But since they have no root, they last only a short time. When trouble or persecution comes because of the word, they quickly fall away. Still others, like seed sown among thorns, hear the word; but the worries of this life, the deceitfulness of wealth and the desires for other things come in and choke the word, making it unfruitful. Others, like seed sown on good

soil, hear the word, accept it, and produce a crop—thirty, sixty or even a hundred times what was sown."

262 Matthew 7:6
"Do not give dogs what is sacred; do not throw your pearls to pigs. If you do, they may trample them under their feet, and then turn and tear you to pieces.

263 2 Samuel 11:27–12:1
After the time of mourning was over, David had her brought to his house, and she became his wife and bore him a son. But the thing David had done displeased the LORD. The LORD sent Nathan to David…

264 Isaiah 14:13–14
You said in your heart, "I will ascend to heaven; I will raise my throne above the stars of God; I will sit enthroned on the mount of assembly, on the utmost heights of the sacred mountain. I will ascend above the tops of the clouds; I will make myself like the Most High."

Endnotes for Caress

265 Romans 2:4
Or do you show contempt for the riches of his kindness, tolerance and patience, not realizing that God's kindness leads you toward repentance?

266 Matthew 20:34
Jesus had compassion on them and touched their eyes. Immediately they received their sight and followed him.

267 2 Peter 3:9
The Lord is not slow in keeping his promise, as some understand slowness. He is patient with you, not wanting anyone to perish, but everyone to come to repentance.

268   Galatians 5:22–23
           But the fruit of the Spirit is love, joy, peace, patience,
           kindness, goodness, faithfulness, gentleness and self-
           control. Against such things there is no law.

269   Hebrews 13:8
           Jesus Christ is the same yesterday and today and forever.

270   Mark 1:41
           Filled with compassion, Jesus reached out his hand and
           touched the man. "I am willing," he said. "Be clean!"

271   Isaiah 55:7
           Let the wicked forsake his way and the evil man his
           thoughts. Let him turn to the LORD, and he will have
           mercy on him, and to our God, for he will freely pardon.

272   John 6:44
           "No one can come to me unless the Father who sent me
           draws him, and I will raise him up at the last day.

273   Mark 16:15
           He said to them, "Go into all the world and preach the
           good news to all creation.

274   Luke 5:13
           Jesus reached out his hand and touched the man. "I am
           willing," he said. "Be clean!"

275   2 Peter 1:3
           His divine power has given us everything we need for
           life and Godliness through our knowledge of him who
           called us by his own glory and goodness.

276   John 12:32
           But I, when I am lifted up from the earth, will draw all
           men to myself."

277   Jeremiah 29:11
       For I know the plans I have for you," declares the Lord,
       "plans to prosper you and not to harm you, plans to give
       you hope and a future.

278   Matthew 17:5
       While he was still speaking, a bright cloud enveloped
       them, and a voice from the cloud said, "This is my Son,
       whom I love; with him I am well pleased. Listen to
       him!"

279   Isaiah 42:3
       A bruised reed he will not break, and a smoldering wick
       he will not snuff out. In faithfulness he will bring forth
       justice;

280   2 Timothy 3:17
       so that the man of God may be thoroughly equipped for
       every good work.

281   Psalm 13:5
       But I trust in your unfailing love; my heart rejoices in
       your salvation.

282   Galatians 5:22–23
       But the fruit of the Spirit is love, joy, peace, patience,
       kindness, goodness, faithfulness, gentleness and self-
       control. Against such things there is no law.

283   Romans 12:2
       Do not conform any longer to the pattern of this world,
       but be transformed by the renewing of your mind. Then
       you will be able to test and approve what God's will
       is—his good, pleasing and perfect will.

284   Romans 7:6
       The Living Bible: But now you need no longer worry
       about the Jewish laws and customs because you "died"

while in their captivity and now you can really serve God; not in the old way, mechanically obeying a set of rules, but in the new way, with all of your hearts and minds.

285   2 Timothy 1:7
           God empowers us to get our flesh into submission: For God did not give us a spirit of timidity, but a spirit of power, of love and of self-discipline.

Endnotes for Offer

286   Luke 11:10
           The offer from God: For everyone who asks receives…

287   Acts 2:38
           The offer of the Holy Spirit: … And you will receive the gift of the Holy Spirit.

288   Hebrews 6:18
           The offer of hope: God did this so that, by two unchangeable things in which it is impossible for God to lie, we who have fled to take hold of the hope offered to us may be greatly encouraged.

289   John 6:51
           I am the living bread that came down from heaven. If anyone eats of this bread, he will live forever. This bread is my flesh, which I will give for the life of the world.”

290   John 10:10
           The thief comes only to steal and kill and destroy; I have come that they may have life, and have it to the full.

291   John 20:22
           The offer of the Holy Spirit: And with that he breathed on them and said, “Receive the Holy Spirit.

292   Acts 1:8
         The offer to give Power: But you will receive power
         when the Holy Spirit comes on you…

293   Galatians 5:22–23
         But the fruit of the Spirit is love, joy, peace, patience,
         kindness, goodness, faithfulness, gentleness and self-
         control. Against such things there is no law.

294   Ephesians 3:20
         The offer of God is more than we can think: Now to
         him who is able to do immeasurably more than all we
         ask or imagine, according to his power that is at work
         within us,

295   Mark 11:24
         The offer of everything: … believe that you have received
         it, and it will be yours.

296   Hebrews 7:27
         The offer of Jesus: … He sacrificed for their sins once
         for all when he offered himself.

297   Jeremiah 29:11–13
         For I know the plans I have for you," declares the LORD,
         "plans to prosper you and not to harm you, plans to give
         you hope and a future. Then you will call upon me and
         come and pray to me, and I will listen to you. You will
         seek me and find me when you seek me with all your
         heart.

298   Ephesians 3:16–19
         I pray that out of his glorious riches he may strengthen
         you with power through his Spirit in your inner being,
         so that Christ may dwell in your hearts through faith.

And I pray that you, being rooted and established in love, may have power, together with all the saints, to grasp how wide and long and high and deep is the love of Christ, and to know this love that surpasses knowledge—that you may be filled to the measure of all the fullness of God.

299 Matthew 21:22
The offer of whatever you ask for: If you believe, you will receive whatever you ask for in prayer."

300 John 16:24
The offer of joy: Ask and you will receive, and your joy will be complete.

301 Revelation 3:20
The offer of relationship: Here I am! I stand at the door and knock. If anyone hears my voice and opens the door, I will come in and eat with him, and he with me.

302 James 1:17
Every good and perfect gift is from above, coming down from the Father of the heavenly lights, who does not change like shifting shadows.

303 Isaiah 30:18
Yet the LORD longs to be gracious to you; he rises to show you compassion. For the LORD is a God of justice. Blessed are all who wait for him!

304 Romans 1:24
Therefore God gave them over in the sinful desires of their hearts to sexual impurity for the degrading of their bodies with one another.

305   Genesis 9:5
           And for your lifeblood I will surely demand an account-
           ing. I will demand an accounting from every animal.
           And from each man, too, I will demand an accounting
           for the life of his fellow man.

306   Psalm 25:10
           All the ways of the LORD are loving and faithful for
           those who keep the demands of his covenant.

307   2 Timothy 3:17
           so that the man of God may be thoroughly equipped for
           every good work.

308   Hebrews 12:2
           Let us fix our eyes on Jesus, the author and perfecter of
           our faith…

309   John 3:16
           "For God so loved the world that he gave his one and
           only Son, that whoever believes in him shall not perish
           but have eternal life.

310   Acts 1:8
           But you will receive power when the Holy Spirit comes
           on you; and you will be my witnesses in Jerusalem, and
           in all Judea and Samaria, and to the ends of the earth."

311   Isaiah 54:2
           "Enlarge the place of your tent, stretch your tent curtains
           wide, do not hold back; lengthen your cords, strengthen
           your stakes.

312   Isaiah 43:19
           See, I am doing a new thing! Now it springs up; do you
           not perceive it? I am making a way in the desert and
           streams in the wasteland.

313   Revelation 3:20
Here I am! I stand at the door and knock. If anyone hears my voice and opens the door, I will come in and eat with him, and he with me.

Endnotes for Bless

314   Malachi 3:10
Bring the whole tithe into the storehouse, that there may be food in my house. Test me in this," says the LORD Almighty, "and see if I will not throw open the floodgates of heaven and pour out so much blessing that you will not have room enough for it.

315   Psalm 29:11
The LORD gives strength to his people; the LORD blesses his people with peace.

316   Proverbs 10:22
The blessing of the LORD brings wealth, and he adds no trouble to it.

317   Psalm 67:1
May God be gracious to us and bless us and make his face shine upon us…

318   Acts 3:26
When God… sent him first to you to bless you by turning each of you from your wicked ways."

319   Ephesians 1:3
…God … has blessed us in the heavenly realms with every spiritual blessing in Christ.

320   Genesis 22:17
I will surely bless you and make your descendants as numerous as the stars…

321 Job 42:12
The Lord blessed the latter part of Job's life more than the first…

322 James 1:17
Every good and perfect gift is from above, coming down from the Father of the heavenly lights, who does not change like shifting shadows.

323 2 Timothy 3:17
…so that the man of God may be thoroughly equipped for every good work.

324 Galatians 5:1
It is for freedom that Christ has set us free. Stand firm, then, and do not let yourselves be burdened again by a yoke of slavery.

325 Hebrews 12:10
… God disciplines us for our good, that we may share in his holiness.

326 Hosea 4:6
my people are destroyed from lack of knowledge. "Because you have rejected knowledge, I also reject you as my priests; because you have ignored the law of your God, I also will ignore your children.

Endnotes for Teach

327 Psalm 25:9
He guides the humble in what is right and teaches them his way.

328 Genesis 15:6
Abram believed the Lord, and he credited it to him as righteousness.

329   Psalm 23:1-6
The LORD is my shepherd, I shall not be in want. He makes me lie down in green pastures, he leads me beside quiet waters, he restores my soul. He guides me in paths of righteousness for his name's sake. Even though I walk through the valley of the shadow of death, I will fear no evil, for you are with me; your rod and your staff, they comfort me. You prepare a table before me in the presence of my enemies. You anoint my head with oil; my cup overflows. Surely goodness and love will follow me all the days of my life, and I will dwell in the house of the LORD forever.

330   Psalm 32:8
I will instruct you and teach you in the way you should go; I will counsel you and watch over you.

331   Mark 4:13–20
The Parable of the Sower: Then Jesus said to them, "Don't you understand this parable? How then will you understand any parable? The farmer sows the word. Some people are like seed along the path, where the word is sown. As soon as they hear it, Satan comes and takes away the word that was sown in them. Others, like seed sown on rocky places, hear the word and at once receive it with joy. But since they have no root, they last only a short time. When trouble or persecution comes because of the word, they quickly fall away. Still others, like seed sown among thorns, hear the word; but the worries of this life, the deceitfulness of wealth and the desires for other things come in and choke the word, making it unfruitful. Others, like seed sown on good soil, hear the word, accept it, and produce a crop— thirty, sixty or even a hundred times what was sown."

332 1 Corinthians 12:28
And in the church God has appointed first of all apostles, second prophets, third teachers, then workers of miracles, also those having gifts of healing, those able to help others, those with gifts of administration, and those speaking in different kinds of tongues.

333 Matthew 23:10
Nor are you to be called 'teacher,' for you have one Teacher, the Christ.

334 2 Timothy 3:17
so that the man of God may be thoroughly equipped for every good work.

335 Luke 10:2
He told them, "The harvest is plentiful, but the workers are few. Ask the Lord of the harvest, therefore, to send out workers into his harvest field.

336 Mark 6:34
…he had compassion on them… So he began teaching them many things.

337 John 7:16
Jesus answered, "My teaching is not my own. It comes from him who sent me.

338 Luke 12:12
for the Holy Spirit will teach you at that time what you should say."

339 John 7:17
If anyone chooses to do God's will, he will find out whether my teaching comes from God or whether I speak on my own.

340   1 John 2:27
        …But as his anointing teaches you about all things…

341   Matthew 23:4
        They tie up heavy loads and put them on men's shoul-
        ders, but they themselves are not willing to lift a finger
        to move them…

342   John 14:23
        Jesus replied, "If anyone loves me, he will obey my
        teaching…

343   John 8:31
        Jesus said, "If you hold to my teaching, you are really my
        disciples.

344   John 5:19
        Jesus gave them this answer: "I tell you the truth, the
        Son can do nothing by himself; he can do only what he
        sees his Father doing, because whatever the Father does
        the Son also does.

345   Mark 4:13–14
        The Parable of the Sower: Then Jesus said to them,
        "Don't you understand this parable? How then will you
        understand any parable? The farmer sows the word.

Endnotes for Mend

346   1 John 1:5
        …God is light; in him there is no darkness at all.

347   Psalm 107:20
        He sent forth his word and healed them; he rescued
        them from the grave.

348   Genesis 15:6
       Abram believed the Lord, and he credited it to him as
       righteousness.

349   Proverbs 4:1
       Listen, my sons, to a father's instruction; pay attention
       and gain understanding

350   Hosea 14:4
       "I will heal their waywardness and love them freely, for
       my anger has turned away from them.

351   Psalm 23:3
       he restores my soul. He guides me in paths of righteous-
       ness for his name's sake.

352   Psalm 147:3
       He heals the brokenhearted…

353   John 10:10
       The thief comes only to steal and kill and destroy; I
       have come that they may have life, and have it to the
       full.

354   Philippians 4:19
       And my God will meet all your needs according to his
       glorious riches in Christ Jesus.

355   1 Corinthians 3:6
       I planted the seed, Apollos watered it, but God made it
       grow.

356   2 Timothy 3:17
       …so that the man of God may be thoroughly equipped
       for every good work.

357   Psalm 34:18
The Lord is close to the brokenhearted and saves those who are crushed in spirit.

358   Matthew 13:15
For this people's heart has become calloused; they hardly hear with their ears, and they have closed their eyes. Otherwise they might see with their eyes, hear with their ears, understand with their hearts and turn, and I would heal them.'

359   Psalm 41:4
I said, "O Lord, have mercy on me; heal me, for I have sinned against you."

360   Mark 4:13–20
Then Jesus said to them, "Don't you understand this parable? How then will you understand any parable? The farmer sows the word. Some people are like seed along the path, where the word is sown. As soon as they hear it, Satan comes and takes away the word that was sown in them. Others, like seed sown on rocky places, hear the word and at once receive it with joy. But since they have no root, they last only a short time. When trouble or persecution comes because of the word, they quickly fall away. Still others, like seed sown among thorns, hear the word; but the worries of this life, the deceitfulness of wealth and the desires for other things come in and choke the word, making it unfruitful. Others, like seed sown on good soil, hear the word, accept it, and produce a crop—thirty, sixty or even a hundred times what was sown."

361   Matthew 7:21–23
"Not everyone who says to me, 'Lord, Lord,' will enter the kingdom of heaven, but only he who does the will of my Father who is in heaven. Many will say to me

on that day, 'Lord, Lord, did we not prophesy in your name, and in your name drive out demons and perform many miracles?' Then I will tell them plainly, 'I never knew you. Away from me, you evildoers!'

362   Romans 12:2
Do not conform any longer to the pattern of this world, but be transformed by the renewing of your mind. Then you will be able to test and approve what God's will is—his good, pleasing and perfect will.

Endnotes for Empower

363   Isaiah 55:8–11
"For my thoughts are not your thoughts, neither are your ways my ways," declares the LORD. "As the heavens are higher than the earth, so are my ways higher than your ways and my thoughts than your thoughts. As the rain and the snow come down from heaven, and do not return to it without watering the earth and making it bud and flourish, so that it yields seed for the Sower and bread for the eater, so is my word that goes out from my mouth: It will not return to me empty, but will accomplish what I desire and achieve the purpose for which I sent it.

364   Luke 24:49
I am going to send you what my Father has promised; but stay in the city until you have been clothed with power from on high."

365   Psalm 127:1
Unless the LORD builds the house, its builders labor in vain. Unless the LORD watches over the city, the watchmen stand guard in vain.

366   James 3:13
        ... Let him show it by his good life, by deeds done in the humility that comes from wisdom.

367   1 John 5:6
        The Spirit is Truth: This is the one who came by water and blood—Jesus Christ. He did not come by water only, but by water and blood. And it is the Spirit who testifies, because the Spirit is the truth.

368   Acts 1:8
        But you will receive power when the Holy Spirit comes on you ...

369   2 Corinthians 10:4
        The weapons we fight with are not the weapons of the world. On the contrary, they have divine power to demolish strongholds.

370   1 Corinthians 2:4
        ...not with wise and persuasive words, but with a demonstration of the Spirit's power,

371   Luke 9:1
        When Jesus had called the Twelve together, he gave them power and authority to drive out all demons and to cure diseases,

372   Galatians 5:22–23
        But the fruit of the Spirit is love, joy, peace, patience, kindness, goodness, faithfulness, gentleness and self-control. Against such things there is no law.

373   Psalm 37:6
        God shows us off: He will make your righteousness shine like the dawn, the justice of your cause like the noonday sun.

374   2 Timothy 3:17
           so that the man of God may be thoroughly equipped for
           every good work.

375   2 Timothy 3:5
           having a form of godliness but denying its power. Have
           nothing to do with them.

376   Mark 12:24
           Jesus replied, "Are you not in error because you do not
           know the Scriptures or the power of God?"

377   2 Timothy 2:15
           Do your best to present yourself to God as one approved,
           a workman who does not need to be ashamed and who
           correctly handles the word of truth.

378   Matthew 28:18–20
           Then Jesus came to them and said, "All authority in
           heaven and on earth has been given to me. Therefore
           go and make disciples of all nations, baptizing them in
           the name of the Father and of the Son and of the Holy
           Spirit, and teaching them to obey everything I have
           commanded you. And surely I am with you always, to
           the very end of the age."

Endnotes for Send

379   Isaiah 6:8
           Then I heard the voice of the Lord saying, "Whom
           shall I send? And who will go for us?" And I said, "Here
           am I. Send me!"

380   Luke 10:3
           Go! I am sending you out like lambs among wolves.

381   Luke 9:2–5
and he sent them out to preach the kingdom of God and to heal the sick. He told them: "Take nothing for the journey—no staff, no bag, no bread, no money, no extra tunic. Whatever house you enter, stay there until you leave that town. If people do not welcome you, shake the dust off your feet when you leave their town, as a testimony against them."

382   Matthew 10:1
Jesus sends out the twelve: He called his twelve disciples to him and gave them authority to drive out evil spirits and to heal every disease and sickness.

383   Luke 10:2
He told them, "The harvest is plentiful, but the workers are few. Ask the Lord of the harvest, therefore, to send out workers into his harvest field."

384   Genesis 16:12
He will be a wild donkey of a man; his hand will be against everyone and everyone's hand against him, and he will live in hostility toward all his brothers."

385   Jeremiah 14:15
Therefore, this is what the Lord says about the prophets who are prophesying in my name: I did not send them, yet they are saying, 'No sword or famine will touch this land.' Those same prophets will perish by sword and famine.

386   Mark 5:25–29
And a woman was there who had been subject to bleeding for twelve years. She had suffered a great deal under the care of many doctors and had spent all she had, yet instead of getting better she grew worse. When she heard about Jesus, she came up behind him in the

crowd and touched his cloak, because she thought, "If I just touch his clothes, I will be healed." Immediately her bleeding stopped and she felt in her body that she was freed from her suffering.

387   Mark 5:41–42
He took her by the hand and said to her, "Talitha koum!" (which means, "Little girl, I say to you, get up!"). Immediately the girl stood up and walked around (she was twelve years old). At this they were completely astonished.

388   Romans 10:14–15
How, then, can they call on the one they have not believed in? And how can they believe in the one of whom they have not heard? And how can they hear without someone preaching to them? And how can they preach unless they are sent? As it is written, "How beautiful are the feet of those who bring good news!"

389   Luke 24:49
I am going to send you what my Father has promised; but stay in the city until you have been clothed with power from on high."

390   2 Timothy 3:17
so that the man of God may be thoroughly equipped for every good work.

391   Matthew 28:18–20
Then Jesus came to them and said, "All authority in heaven and on earth has been given to me. Therefore go and make disciples of all nations, baptizing them in the name of the Father and of the Son and of the Holy Spirit, and teaching them to obey everything I have commanded you. And surely I am with you always, to the very end of the age."

392   John 20:21
        Again Jesus said, "Peace be with you! As the Father has
        sent me, I am sending you."

393   John 10:10
        The thief comes only to steal and kill and destroy; I
        have come that they may have life, and have it to the
        full.

394   1 Corinthians 7:32–35
        I would like you to be free from concern. An unmarried
        man is concerned about the Lord's affairs—how he can
        please the Lord. But a married man is concerned about
        the affairs of this world—how he can please his wife—
        and his interests are divided. An unmarried woman or
        virgin is concerned about the Lord's affairs: her aim is
        to be devoted to the Lord in both body and spirit. But
        a married woman is concerned about the affairs of this
        world—how she can please her husband. I am saying
        this for your own good, not to restrict you, but that you
        may live in a right way in undivided devotion to the
        Lord.

395   Malachi 2:15
        Has not the LORD made them one? In flesh and spirit
        they are his. And why one? Because he was seeking
        godly offspring. So guard yourself in your spirit, and do
        not break faith with the wife of your youth.

396   Romans 11:29
        for God's gifts and his call are irrevocable.

Endnotes for Expanding the Servant Process

397 Romans 10:14–15
How, then, can they call on the one they have not believed in? And how can they believe in the one of whom they have not heard? And how can they hear without someone preaching to them? And how can they preach unless they are sent? As it is written, "How beautiful are the feet of those who bring good news!"

Endnotes for Expanding the deception process

398 Matthew 16:17
Jesus replied, "Blessed are you, Simon son of Jonah, for this was not revealed to you by man, but by my Father in heaven.

399 Proverbs 14:12
There is a way that seems right to a man, but in the end it leads to death.

400 Proverbs 30:15–16
…There are three things that are never satisfied, four that never say, 'Enough!': the grave, the barren womb, land, which is never satisfied with water, and fire, which never says, 'Enough!'

401 Hosea 4:6
my people are destroyed from lack of knowledge…

Endnotes for Closing Statement

402 Luke 23:40–43
But the other criminal rebuked him. "Don't you fear God," he said, "since you are under the same sentence? We are punished justly, for we are getting what our

deeds deserve. But this man has done nothing wrong."
Then he said, "Jesus, remember me when you come
into your kingdom." Jesus answered him, "I tell you the
truth, today you will be with me in paradise."

403   James 2:18
        But someone will say, "You have faith; I have deeds."
        Show me your faith without deeds, and I will show you
        my faith by what I do.

404   1 Corinthians 3:7–8
        So neither he who plants nor he who waters is anything,
        but only God, who makes things grow. The man who
        plants and the man who waters have one purpose, and
        each will be rewarded according to his own labor.

405   Matthew 25:23
        "His master replied, 'Well done, good and faithful ser-
        vant! You have been faithful with a few things; I will
        put you in charge of many things. Come and share your
        master's happiness!'

406   1 John 3:2
        Dear friends, now we are children of God, and what we
        will be has not yet been made known. But we know that
        when he appears, we shall be like him, for we shall see
        him as he is.

407   Matthew 28:18–20
        Then Jesus came to them and said, "All authority in
        heaven and on earth has been given to me. Therefore
        go and make disciples of all nations, baptizing them in
        the name of the Father and of the Son and of the Holy
        Spirit, and teaching them to obey everything I have
        commanded you. And surely I am with you always, to
        the very end of the age."